DARING
TO BE GREAT

*"People do not decide to become extraordinary.
They decide to accomplish extraordinary things."*
- Edmund Hillary

DARING TO BE GREAT

HOW TO OUTSELL THE MOST FEROCIOUS
COMPETITION IN YOUR MARKETPLACE, EVEN
WHEN THEIR MARKETING IS BRILLIANT
AND THEIR BUDGETS ARE HUGE.

MATT BERRY

First edition

ISBN: 978-0-473-55100-1

Cover Design: Michael Rehder

Illustrations: Daniela Pelle

Cover Photography: Richard Parsonson

DEDICATION

This book is the result of my own business changing and forcing me to find a better way. It's been a messy but necessary process. And while that change wasn't easy or enjoyable, it does bring me immeasurable fulfilment to share what I learned as a result of those challenges.

I want to thank my family, who both endure and endlessly support me while I pursue my entrepreneurial calling.

To my three beautiful children (Mikaela, Mason & Miller), thank you for believing in me. I hope you're as proud of me as I am of you.

To my wife, Tina. You deserve all the credit for the person - and businessperson - I've become. Without your love and support, none of this would have been possible. Nor would any of it matter.

TABLE OF CONTENTS

THIS METHODOLOGY IS DIFFERENT

In this book, I'm going to reveal a pioneering marketing and sales methodology that you've probably never heard of before. Many will consider it highly controversial. Not because it's untrue, it's just unlike anything that they've been taught before.

I don't mind people thinking it's contentious. That simply reflects that this approach is not commonplace. And that's a good thing because right now that provides a distinct competitive advantage.

As you'll learn in this book, building a rapidly growing business is a progression of steps. Some days progress will feel slow, while other days you'll be dealing with such rapid growth you'll feel like your spinning out of control. This is normal.

But I must warn you, as you break away from conventional thinking, here's what's going to happen. At first, people will notice that you're doing something different. Then they'll start questioning your decisions. And finally, they'll start telling you that you'd be better off doing what everyone else has always done.

As with anything new you're not going to get it perfect straight away, but as soon as your results start to show their attitudes will change. They'll stop asking why you're doing what you do, and instead, will start asking you how you do it, so that they can get what you've got.

That is how greatness is achieved. It's pushing pass the norm because conventional approaches will only ever produce conventional results. History proves this time and time again.

"First, they ignore you.
Then they laugh at you.
Then they fight you.
Then you win."
- Mahatma Gandhi

'Daring to be great' is a challenge for all entrepreneurs and business owners. Too many of us are struggling and failing. And while we can't always control the hand we're dealt in business; we're in complete control of deciding if we want to be more than we are right now.

All of us have the potential for greatness, but first, we must choose to be great.

Make a decision. That doesn't mean you're going to succeed today. It doesn't even mean you're going to be good at it today. But strive for greatness every day.

Greatness is simply doing more than we ever imagined we were capable of. It's moving beyond our own status quo through sacrifice, dedication, time, effort and much more.

You can have it all. You just need to find the greatness inside of you.

CHAPTER 1

INTRODUCTION

When you started your business, the prospect of growth must have seemed exhilarating. An entrepreneur's whole psyche is founded on forward momentum – it's baked deep into our DNA and it fuels our sense of possibility.

Coming up with brilliant products and services is rarely an issue, but when our businesses aren't growing as quickly as we'd envisioned, it's natural to seek a better way. For most entrepreneurs, however, that manifests itself as doing more of the same thing – buying more advertising, building a bigger website or knocking on a few more doors – and in truth, the results are likely to reflect the rise and fall of the economy and nothing more. Such approaches boil down to playing it safe. Yet calculated risk-taking is a mandatory part of success.

What many entrepreneurs don't realise is that by playing it safe, they're just as likely, if not more so, to put their company in harm's way. The risks include missed opportunities, flat-to-declining performance, customer churn and employee turnover. Even if you avoid such extreme outcomes, the worst feeling an entrepreneur can experience is to settle for a shrinking vision of what their business could be.

Whether you're a fledgling start-up or have been chipping away for many years, intuitively the most efficient way to produce a phenomenal result is to replicate a phenomenal business. Then again, if you were to model yourself on someone in your local market, all you'd be doing is playing it safe.

Consider too that if you're going to replicate a growth model, then it might as well be the world's fastest-growing companies, because they're clearly doing something phenomenal. It won't surprise you to learn that these are mammoth technology-based companies such as Airbnb, Facebook and Uber.

It may seem hard to believe, but there was a time when Airbnb was for travellers who were happy to crash on an airbed at the founder's apartment. Or when Facebook was an online community for Harvard students, or when the plan for Uber was to create a timeshare limo service.

How did powerhouses like these evolve from such humble beginnings? It wasn't just by wishing they would catch on, I assure you. There's a rigorous methodology behind their extraordinary rise that until recently was known to very few.

At its core, that methodology – which internet entrepreneur Sean Ellis labelled "growth hacking" in 2010 – is a singular, unrelenting focus on growth.

Success born from failure

Growth hacking confronts the critical challenge of how a business can expand its customer base as fast and as cost-efficiently as possible. Ironically, it owes its existence to the failure of some of the world's best marketing minds.

You see, initially these start-ups tried to achieve rapid growth by hiring veteran marketers. But there was a massive disconnect. Traditional marketing is expensive – especially when your goal is to acquire millions of customers worldwide. So, when these marketers failed to hit their customer-acquisition goals (while also exhausting their budgets), it occurred to the start-ups that they needed a better way. In essence, they were forced to reinvent the process of marketing and expanding their businesses.

When growth hacking started to take shape as a new business discipline, it highlighted how outdated traditional marketing tactics had become. In fact, the age of 90% of the most deployed marketing tactics ranged from several decades to well over a century. Hence, the core principle of "experimentation" was introduced, which involves the rapid conceptualisation, deployment and evaluation of potential growth ideas. As soon as these start-ups began achieving better results, at a fraction of the cost of traditional methods, they knew they were on to something special.

At first glance, you might be concerned that the success of these global tech companies will have little relevance to your own efforts, but it's the underlying framework that holds the value. If your goal is to rapidly double your sales, or even increase them tenfold, this framework can help you achieve that. After all, growth hacking derives its results from customer acquisition and the monetisation and retention of those customers. These methods can be applied to any business you can imagine, from doctors to dog walkers, regardless of their size or marketing budget.

This book contains all the knowledge you need to attract a predictable, consistent flow of new customers into your business every month. But to be clear, it isn't specifically about growth hacking. In fact, if I were to take you through the entire growth-hacking framework, I doubt it would benefit you much. It's too broad a topic and you'd be overwhelmed with irrelevant information.

Instead, I've deconstructed the growth phenomenon that is enabling start-ups to beat out billion-dollar brands. I've also isolated the components that are delivering the best results to form the most effective selling system in modern business.

In the loop

The system I reveal is called a growth loop. I was first introduced to this through Brian Balfour, a noted growth pioneer, who realised that traditional growth models ignored the compounding effects from growth itself. In other words, they failed to account for how an acquired customer could lead to the acquisition of more customers. And while the mechanics of how I approach growth loops are completely different from Brian's, our frameworks share the same objective: to create a self-sustaining growth system that can exponentially boost your business.

Growth loops are not an easy fix, a silver bullet or a clever gimmick. In truth, they require a lot more effort than traditional approaches, but the payoff is that much more impressive.

Before we begin, however, I must mentally prepare you for something.

You need to be willing to rethink how your business grows because inevitably, you'll need to change what you've been doing. And with anything new, your first reaction will be one of uncertainty. We're all conditioned to revert to the status quo, as that's what we're most comfortable with. But comfort is a death sentence when it comes to progress.

It's a simple equation: you can't play it safe and expect things to change significantly.

However, if you're ready to go all in and push through those inevitable moments of doubt, buying this book may be one of the smartest decisions of your life.

Wherever you are on your journey, I hope it helps you.

Let's get started.

CHAPTER 2

HOPE IS NOT A STRATEGY

If you're like most entrepreneurs, you're working much longer hours, suffering more stress and taking less time off than when you worked for someone else. And while I hate to be the bearer of bad news, your business is probably going to fail.

An estimated 96% of businesses will fail within ten years, but perhaps what's scarier is that the majority are only ever 27 days away from permanently closing.

When a business does collapse, the reason most commonly cited is that it ran out of cash. But trust me, the cracks in those businesses started well before the day they closed. You see, businesses run out on money all the time. In fact, some run out of money multiple times a week, yet they're still here.

Only one thing kills a business and that's the founder giving up. The moment they decide they can't keep fighting for its survival is the moment it all ends.

But here's the thing. If they had found a way to build an enduring business, they wouldn't have needed to give up on their dream. So, it's fair to conclude that the only difference between a business collapsing or thriving is its ability to grow.

I often work with intelligent, hardworking people whose businesses are struggling because they haven't invested in growth. They don't know how much will be "too much" or how little will be "too little" or, in a lot of cases, where to even begin. So, they opt to do the absolute minimum or, worse, nothing at all.

What differentiates the fastest-growing companies from everyone else is that they're not afraid to invest a massive amount in growth. If you look at the top ten tech companies worth over $1 billion, the average enterprise will spend $0.72 on sales and marketing for every $1 they made back in their first three years.

Not investing in growth produces a business that has an unpredictable and unreliable flow of customers coming into it. Ultimately, you're left hoping that everything works out. It's a vain hope, I'm afraid.

So, why do so many entrepreneurs think their business won't fail? Well, this might sound harsh, but entrepreneurs inherently have a narcissistic trait. They believe that if their product or service is better than their competitors, then all that business stuff will take care of itself. It doesn't work that way, sadly – at least, not any more.

That "build it and they will come" mindset hails from a time when small towns had one provider of each business type servicing their local community: one bank, one supermarket, one barber, etc. And so, in an environment where there was little or no competition, opening a store meant the customers had to come to you. You were their only choice.

These days we operate in a hyper-competitive global market, competing against a daunting number of businesses – which means: "If you build it, they don't care and they'll only come if you market yourself."

The level of competition is so intense that at some stage, your business will hit a growth ceiling where sales begin to plateau. Growth ceilings occur in every business – and as a firm grows, it can hit multiple growth ceilings along the way, at multiple stages.

Pushing through these ceilings always requires a fundamental shift, as the business you have is not the business that will rocket you through this barrier. Sadly, though, I'm forever seeing entrepreneurs attempting to do just that, and in pursuit of growth, they will all make the same three mistakes.

GROWTH CEILINGS

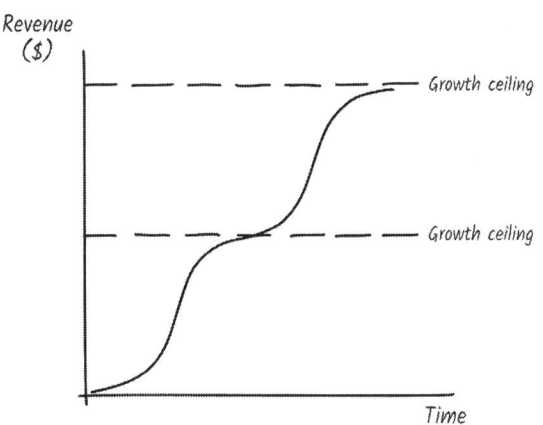

Errors to avoid

The first mistake is that they'll start working longer hours and personally try to produce more. This constant dollars-for-hours trade-off rarely allows them to achieve their vision of growth. In the end, they'll decide that working hard is not that sustainable, so they'll move on to their second mistake, which is to hire additional staff.

Bear in mind that every time a business employs someone, it becomes less financially efficient. Invariably the entrepreneur has to sacrifice the business's short-term profitability or take a pay cut to fund their staffing initiative. Each option leaves the entrepreneur questioning their choice, but with the extra staff on board, they then fool themselves into thinking everything will be OK if they can run a bit more efficiently.

Then along comes their third mistake. They invest in the latest technology and equipment to improve their margins. However, in most cases, these businesses will never see a return on this investment; if they do, it tends to be only in the short term. Before they know it, they're back investing in the next round of the latest and greatest technology to improve their margins again.

So, what's the way forward? To grow your business rapidly, you'll certainly need to work harder, employ staff and invest in technology, but these are all very much secondary tasks. The most crucial step is to create a selling system first.

Sales, sales, sales

The number-one rule in business growth is "sales eclipse everything else". When your business is engulfed with a consistent stream of profitable sales, there's practically no problem that can't be solved, no one you can't hire and no equipment you can't buy. That's why establishing a selling system like the one I outline is the key to a successful business.

Your business's existence depends on how effective you are at generating sales. Consider the difference between (i) a builder who starts a building company but struggles each year to secure enough projects and (ii) a builder who creates a massive construction enterprise. The difference lies not in their ability to build, but to market and sell their services.

To be a genuinely effective entrepreneur, you must be your business's number-one sales expert. That doesn't mean you have to be the one who's selling, or building the website, or writing copy for your ads, but it does mean that you need to design every step of your process so that you can understand it and identify the opportunities that will lead to gains.

You're going to need to divert a significant amount of your time and focus to it too, because I can guarantee you you're not spending anywhere enough time on it presently.

No matter which industry you're in, you'll be busy working "in" your business rather than "on" your business. I say that with confidence, because nearly all business is started by the "craftsman".

The craftsman is someone who has mastered a skillset over time through education and experience and decides one day that they'd like to run a business.

We recently had a builder doing some work on our house, and I asked him what had driven him to set up on his own. He explained that after securing his first building qualifications, he got an apprenticeship and worked for someone else for several years. Eventually, he decided to back himself and go out independently.

That is how the vast majority of businesses start. And while they're able to make a living off their skillsets, there's always one big chink in their armour. Doing your job and building a business are entirely different skillsets.

Ask any craftsman how much training they've had on running a successful business and the likely answer will be little or none. Sure, they try to figure it all out as best they can, but very few have ever been taught how to acquire customers or make their firm stand out from the crowd.

If you're serious about growing a business, there's one thing that you need to realise. You need to be across how it generates (or could generate) its revenue and then ensure that the correct systems are in place to deliver against your growth plans. Otherwise, you'll be flying in the dark, hoping that things work out.

CHAPTER 3
GROWTH MODELLING

"So… what exactly is a growth loop?" the business owner asked.

It's a question I'm asked almost daily, and I've spent countless hours trying to come up with an answer that's both concise and impressive. Fruitlessly, as it happens.

"A growth loop is a self-sustaining growth system that continuously builds upon itself."

I paused, knowing that my response didn't answer the question adequately.

"It's a framework that creates exponential growth through its ability to make greater gains than the effort required to generate them," I added quickly.

That didn't work either.

"Ahh… it's a selling process that makes you loads of money, fast," I said optimistically.

"Now I like the sound of that. I need a growth loop!" came the reply.

Just like businesses, growth loops are complex, multi-faceted entities. The first description I gave – of a self-sustaining system that continuously builds upon itself – is 100% correct, but without an understanding of how it does that, or why it's important, it's devoid of any meaningful context. With that in mind, we need to understand where growth loops emerged from by stepping back and considering traditional growth modelling.

Linear, logarithmic and exponential growth

The three growth models that successful business-es are most likely to follow are linear, logarithmic and exponential. I'll explain each one in turn, but let's just say that everyone dreams of exponential growth, ex-pects to achieve linear growth and will probably end up with the logarithmic kind.

GROWTH MODELS

Exponential   Linear   Logarithmic

Linear growth sits in the middle of these three growth models and is defined by the expectation that a business will continuously grow at the same rate, year after year.

While some businesses do achieve this, the vast majority eventually hit a growth ceiling that impacts their aspirations. You might say this is inevitable, be-cause as a business grows, it becomes more chaotic. As a result, it is harder and more expensive to achieve continuous growth.

This is why most businesses end up following the logarithmic growth model. For a good illustration of this, imagine that you go running 5 kilometres every day and you chart your progress.

LOGARITHMIC GROWTH

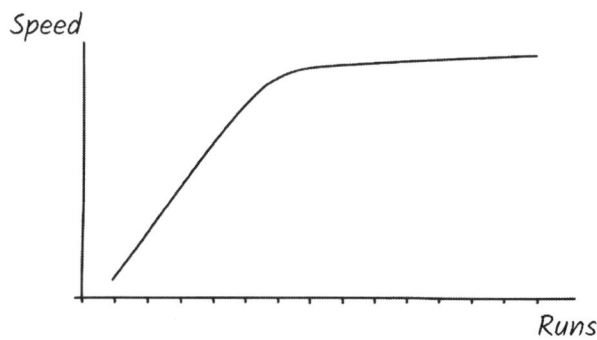

As you begin building up your fitness levels you will be able to complete each run in a shorter time frame by increasing your speed. But eventually you will approach the maximum speed that you can physically run at, and from there it becomes harder and harder to make improvements. That's your growth ceiling.

This explains why elite athletes spend enormous amounts of time and effort training, to shave fractions of a second off their best time. By contrast, a novice runner can initially shave seconds off their best time simply by turning up and trying to do better than their last run.

The challenge for a business facing a logarithmic growth pattern is that once they've hit a growth ceiling, they don't know how to kickstart their growth again. Instead they plod along, hoping things will improve.

Compare that situation with a business experiencing exponential growth – an enviable position to be in. It's the rarest of the three models but will outperform the others every time.

To illustrate exponential growth, let's say you created a social media platform. It's very small to begin with, but as it becomes more popular, it grows more and more quickly. Eventually, every action you take leads to more gains at a faster rate. What's fascinating, though, is how disproportionate the gains become in comparison to the effort you put in.

EXPONENTIAL GROWTH

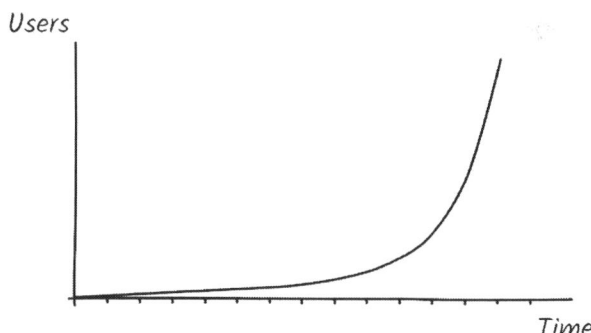

Think of it this way: while a logarithmic curve that's hit a growth ceiling might need 20% more effort to achieve a 2% overall gain, an exponential curve might need 2% more effort to achieve a 20% gain.

In short, this is the foundation of growth loops. A loop of this kind provides exponential growth by enabling greater gains than the effort required to generate them.

Funnel versus loop

Until now, the most adopted sales framework has been the sales funnel, invented in 1898 by advertising pioneer Elias St Elmo Lewis. It's been a cornerstone of marketing strategy ever since.

A sales funnel represents each of the stages a customer goes through. The premise is that you drive traffic into the top of the funnel, typically through advertising, some of this awareness will convert into leads, some of the leads will convert into prospects, and you end up with customers emerging from the base.

THE SALES FUNNEL

Funnels are a great starting point and after more than a century of use, they're far from obsolete. But as frameworks go, they're inadequate in the sense that they don't account for self-sustainable growth.

The issue with a traditional funnel is the notion that if you attract a certain amount of prospects into the top of the funnel, then a certain amount of customers will drop out of the bottom. And because there's some truth in that, over time, businesses increasingly focus on the top of the funnel, typically by advertising more.

The snag is that supporting increased activity at the top of the funnel needs more and more money. That's where the funnel stalls, because no one has an endless supply of cash. Ultimately, a business can expand only as quickly as its marketing budgets will allow.

But growth loops are different.

Growth loops account for the compounding effects of growth itself.

Everyone's heard of the snowball effect, in which a snowball picks up more snow as it rolls down a hillside, gaining mass and momentum in the process.

It's a metaphor for a cycle that builds upon itself at an increasingly fast rate, which is what you want your business to do: to grow more strongly by feeding off its own growth.

With growth loops, all or part of whatever comes out the bottom of the funnel is reinvested at the top. There's a funnel that you can optimise, but now it has a compounding system attached – so you end up with a self-sustaining system that continuously builds upon itself.

Here's an example. Say a business spends its marketing budget using a traditional sales funnel and acquires 1,000 new customers. Once that's spent, the business can't continue growing until a new marketing budget is approved.

Alternatively, if that business had set up a growth loop, it would be able to regenerate its marketing budget without a single additional cent. We'll examine how it achieves this in the chapters that follow, but the net result is that as the budget is regenerated, you gain the ability to spend it over and over again.

How fast your loop can regenerate your marketing budget is called your earn-back period. The shorter your earn-back period, the sooner you can spend it again. If you're able to get it down to a month, then you can repeatedly spend the same budget 12 times a year. That is why growth loops are the most exciting development in marketing since the funnel.

So, let's talk tactics...

CHAPTER 4

GROWTH LOOPS

D id you know that there are only three ways to grow your sales? They're so obvious, yet the first time I was told them, my reaction was: "Wow, that's amazing!".

They're not a breakthrough in modern thinking, but they do make growth seem straightforward.

The three ways to grow are:

1. Get more customers.

2. Get your customers to buy more frequently.

3. Get your customers to buy higher-priced products/services.

Simple, right?

Thinking about growth and how we're going to achieve it can be a complex, overwhelming task. But the plain truth is that it's the process of improving the acquisition, monetisation and retention of customers.

This is why a growth loop consists of an acquisition loop, a monetisation loop and a retention loop. All are intrinsically linked, reflecting the self-sustaining nature of this methodology.

The contrast between conventional thinking and a growth loop can largely be seen in this looping structure. Traditionally, acquisition and retention are largely considered unrelated tasks, or at best minimally connected because at some point in time, you'll try to retain an acquired customer.

GROWTH LOOP

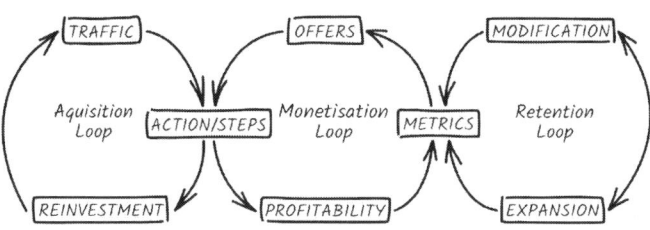

But growth loops see these activities as intrinsically linked. Remember, the growth loop is obsessed with figuring out how we can use growth to obtain more growth. The expectation is that your acquisition efforts must not only lead to greater acquisition, but also support greater retention. Likewise, your retention efforts should not only lead to greater retention, but also support greater acquisition… as you're making a ton of money.

And while it's this infinite looping that will drive your rapid growth, that relies on the strength and contribution of your individual acquisition, monetisation and retention loops.

Each loop has a critical role to play.

The acquisition loop's purpose is to attract a regular supply of new customers. As a standalone loop, its job is to replenish your marketing funds through a series of planned actions/steps, which are then reinvested into acquiring even more customers.

The monetisation loop takes your proprietary offers and guides the customer from one to the next, so you can increase the frequency and value you derive from each customer. While keeping the business afloat, these profits are also reinvested to keep improving the quality of your products or services.

The retention loop, which I'll be coming to in a later chapter, involves keeping your paying customers around for longer. That might sound banal, but its effects on acquisition and profitability are more powerful than you'd think.

It's worth noting too that just as you can run multiple advertising campaigns, you can have numerous acquisition, monetisation and retention loops running simultaneously.

In addition to having multiple growth loops running, the most successful businesses continually develop and deploy new growth loops over time. This is because growth loops also have a growth ceiling, where the loop will become exhausted.

Now, exhaustion has numerous causes – but two common mistakes bring it on quicker.

The first is not understanding how your business grows. If that's the case, then you're forced to test everything just to see if it works or not. Rolling out loops in a haphazard fashion will lead to exhaustion more quickly, because they weren't suitable in the first place.

The second is trying to deploy too many loops at the same time. The wisest approach is to start with one or two, achieve growth and add more over time.

CHAPTER 5
THE BUYER PYRAMID

Contrary to what you've been told, none of the marketing tactics you've been taught will give you the rapid growth you're seeking. It's a big call, I know. And while I'm sure you'll have some success, I know you'll also waste a lot of money achieving it.

The stark truth is that 97% of customers that see your advertising will not buy from you. Marketing and advertising gurus won't tell you that, of course – either because they don't know it, or they're keeping that fact to themselves.

John Wanamaker (1838-1922), founder of one of the United States' first department stores, was a marketing pioneer. "Half the money I spend on advertising is wasted," he famously remarked. "The trouble is, I don't know which half."

As advertising's effectiveness carries on plummeting these days, that figure of half sounds attractive. Yet, naïvely, clients keep spending their budgets on an imprecise relationship. "We advertised last week and our sales increased, so it must have worked," they tell themselves.

And there's the catch: it does work, but not as well as it used to. More to the point, it can't magically persuade someone to whip out their credit card and buy when they're not ready.

Advertising works because it targets easy customers who were going to make a purchase anyway. The challenge was to convince them to buy from you instead of your competitor.

THE BUYER PYRAMID

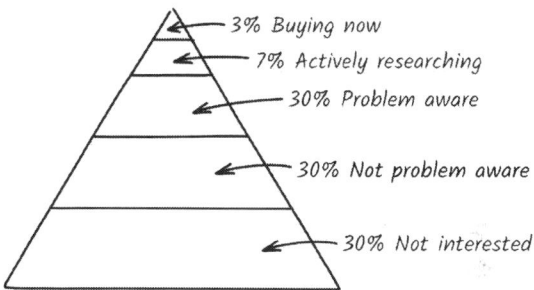

Whenever you pick up the newspaper and see "this weekend only" or switch on the radio and hear "we won't be beaten on price", you know they're going after those easy customers.

In his bestselling book "The Ultimate Sales Machine", Chet Holmes exposed advertising's critical flaw after polling thousands of people. He found that in any given market, at any given time, only 3% of customers are in "buy now" mode. Don't forget too that those 3% are also eyeing your competitors. Suddenly, making the massive profits you've dreamed of looks like an even more daunting challenge.

The good news comes when you look further down the buyer pyramid – because it turns out that the real money sits within the two tiers of customers that aren't even buyers yet.

On closer examination, you'll see that immediately below the 3% in "buy now" mode sits another 7%

of your market. These are actively researching their pending purchase but don't have their wallets out just yet. And below that tier sits a further 30%, who are problem-aware but haven't initiated any actions.

Together, these two tiers account for 37% of your market. That's 12 times larger than the portion of the market everyone else is targeting, yet your competitors ignore them. Why? Because they don't know how to deal with them, simple as that. Their businesses are geared exclusively towards those in "buy now" mode, so they overlook everyone else.

And in doing so, they've missed an enormous opportunity. You, on the other hand, are going to reach out to that 37% and start chipping away at whatever's holding them back from buying.

As you reduce their uncertainty, you'll add so much value upfront that the minute they're ready to buy, your business will be at the top of their list. By then it won't matter how much your competitors scream "buy from me" in their advertising, because you're the one that has built a relationship and positioned yourself to secure a sale.

Here's an important tip, however. You can't treat them like buyers, because they're not quite there yet.

CHAPTER 6
BUILDING TRUST

People in a state of uncertainty don't buy. Period.

That might sound elementary, but you wouldn't believe how many smart, educated business owners and entrepreneurs don't understand it. Customers don't spend 40 hours a week thinking about your products and services the way you do. So, what may seem obvious to you isn't obvious to them.

You need to realise that they're coming to you because you're the expert in your chosen field. They don't have that same expertise. What's more, they won't progress to "buy now" mode until you've reduced or removed their uncertainty.

In a recent study, a neuroeconomist – part of a new interdisciplinary field that looks at how economic decision-making happens inside the brain – imaged subjects' brains as they were forced to make increasingly difficult decisions. As their uncertainty increased, the subjects' brains yielded control over to their limbic system, where emotions such as anxiety and fear are generated.

This brain quirk worked extremely well when we were cave-dwellers who didn't know who or what might be lurking behind the bushes. An overriding sense of caution ensured our survival and explains why our brains are hardwired to react to uncertainty with fear. But this is also why, before any purchase, we consciously and subconsciously evaluate what information we need to overcome our fear and reduce our uncertainty.

The evaluation process behind low-involvement purchases such as buying a cup of coffee is so simple that most of us barely think of it as a decision, and so very little information needs to be collected. High-involvement purchases such as buying a house or car are a different matter altogether, with potential buyers demanding extensive information.

Think about the questions you asked yourself last time you bought a car.

- Which model should I buy?
- How much will it cost?
- What is the safety rating?
- Which colour should I choose?
- What sort of warranties come with the car?
- And so on...

You may not have been consciously aware of it, but until these questions were adequately answered or deemed irrelevant, you would not have made a purchase decision.

The same principle applies to the 37% of your market who are gearing up to become buyers. Consciously and subconsciously, they're collecting information to help them make a purchase decision. Asking for a price, for instance, shows they're trying to reduce their uncertainty around affordability and value.

As a business owner, you can reduce uncertainty in two ways: through information, which helps the customer comprehend your offering; and experience, which occurs when they use your product or engage with your service. In each instance, the underlying foundation of your relationship with them – trust – is strengthened.

Customers have more options than ever when choosing what to purchase – so in a fiercely competitive environment, trust has become a vital differentiator. In all honesty, it has never been more important.

However, as entrepreneurs and business owners, we have a long way to go, given that only 34% of consumers trust the brands they use. Fortunately, the benefits are enormous when we gain a customer's trust. Our brand is the first they'll turn to when making a purchase decision, and when necessary they'll advocate for us and defend our reputation.

Crucially, trust doesn't happen by accident. It's a result of proving that you are trustworthy, which always takes time and effort. Consequently, you need to view building trust as an ongoing obligation to your customers, achieved in small, incremental steps. And as the trust grows, customers will become more comfortable with making larger commitments to you.

As the following graph shows, a prospect's uncertainty levels will be high the first time they encounter our business. Our challenge is to move them along in incremental steps that enable us to reduce this.

With each step, we have a chance to prove our trustworthiness by fulfilling our promises and obligations. And as their uncertainty reduces, trust levels grow correspondingly.

UNCERTAINTY vs TRUST

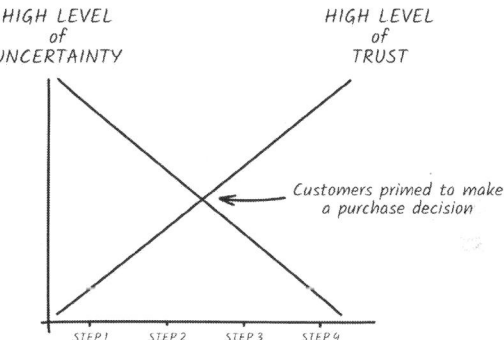

The intersection of the uncertainty and trust lines reflects the point at which the customer is primed to make a purchase decision. Pitching a sales offer before your customer reaches this point is an expensive and futile exercise, as they're simply not ready to bite.

We need to move away from the notion of having to "sell immediately" to the idea of "getting customers ready". The fact that they're not ready to buy right now doesn't mean they'll feel that way in three or six months. So, instead of asking too much, too soon, and losing the opportunity to build your trustworthiness, you should be doing the right thing at the right time.

Asking too much, too soon, is a fundamental problem with almost all marketing and sales campaigns. Research shows that more than 60% of sales are made on the fourth contact, but by that time, 94% of salespeople have given up and moved on to the next prospect.

As you roll out your growth loop, you'll find that you will only need to spend a fraction of your time selling and closing deals. It's your growth loop that will be actively acquiring new clients for you, which in turn allows you to focus on understanding the customer's challenges, offering value and building relationships.

This, as you will find out, pays huge dividends – because by the time the customer has decided to buy, most of your competitors have disappeared. Meanwhile, you have cultivated an enduring, trustworthy relationship with your customers. In no time at all, they'll be banging on your door, insisting you take their money.

CHAPTER 7

HIGH VALUE
CONTENT OFFERS

One of the most effective strategies to build trust is to be of service to others. If you help people in a way that provides you with no immediate benefit, the gains in terms of trust are massive. Being kind goes a long way.

Kindness includes everything from words of advice, pointing them in the right direction, to helping them identify a possible solution. However, taking on responsibility for their problem isn't kind at all – because when you solve it for them, they don't get to learn and grow. On top of that, you must ensure that when you're being kind to others, you aren't being unkind to yourself. All sort of business issues are competing for your attention already. You don't want to take on more commitments, as that will only make matters worse for you.

That's why the first stage of the acquisition loop is based exclusively on the provision of information. And the best part is, you'll produce this content once and run it as an effortlessly distributed automated campaign that requires no further involvement.

This content, called your high-value content offer (HVCO), contains educational material that explains how the customer solves the problem they're grappling with.

HVCOs rely on the concept of reciprocity: the idea that when you provide something of value for free, your customers will feel somewhat indebted to you. So, when they're deciding who to purchase from in the future, they're exponentially more likely to pick you.

HVCOs come in numerous formats, the most common being free ebooks, videos, articles, reports, etc. But whatever form they take, the goal is to move your prospects towards the intersection of uncertainty and trust so that they are primed to receive an offer from you.

Think of it like this. Currently, when your best salesperson has an opportunity with a prospective client, they'll drive out the client's office and answer their questions for an hour. Then they'll get back In their car and drive to the next prospective client.

Inevitably, 90% of the questions that the first prospective client asked will be raised by the second one. So, by capturing your best salesperson responses as content, an HVCO saves an awful lot of time.

Here's what's really magic, however. While your salesperson might fit in six meetings a day, your HVCO can be distributed to 50, or 500, or even 5,000 prospective clients a day! If you've ever wished for a quantum shift in how you generate fresh business leads, this is it.

To build your HVCO, the challenge is to identify the questions that your customers are desperately seeking answers to. We achieve that through a technique called conversational sequencing, which means writing down all the questions a prospective customer has asked, or could ask, about your products or services.

- How does it work?
- How much does it cost?

- What's the delivery timeline?
- Does it come in blue?
- Can I return it?
- How can I try it?
- And so on...

Once you have compiled your questions, you then rank them in order of importance and sequence. For instance, if 90% of your customers ask you about price, how your product works and what the delivery timelines are, then it's fair to assume these factors rank highly in their decision-making.

Be sure also to consider the sequence in which the questions are asked, because sometimes a particular piece of information is of foremost importance. For example, the customer may need some understanding of the cost, even if it's only a rough estimate, before they start to consider finer details like delivery timeframes or warranties.

Once you've worked out your customers' pressing questions, you'll need to create an HVCO. Generally speaking, the best-performing HVCO will be a free report, ebook or video that answers between five and seven burning questions depending on the complexity of your product or service.

You'd be surprised at what goes into some HVCOs. One of our clients with an electrician business made videos about their most common jobs. When they showed prospective clients the entire process, sales soared, because they'd dealt with any uncertainty about the complexity of the project.

Customers had no intention of doing the job themselves (which would be illegal anyway), but the videos showed them exactly what the electrician would do, giving them the confidence to proceed.

In a nutshell, that's the benefit you get from your HVCO. You've proved that you're capable of helping them before you even sign them up as a client, and by the time you present a sales offer, you've already answered their most important questions: "Can I trust them?" and "Will this work?"

I can't stress this enough: this is one of the greatest approaches to generating leads. Some maths will show you want I mean.

Say you run an accountancy business, and you place advertisements that result in 100 people visiting your website. Of those 100, let's say three book in for a meet-and-greet that allows you to present your firm and its services. Then, from those meetings, you achieve a 30% close rate, meaning you've secured one new client.

Now imagine that you still drive 100 people to your website, but this time to exchange their contact details for your HVCO. Because this is based on educating them, rather than selling something to them, your offer converts at a much higher rate, say 30%. As a result, you have 30 prospects that you can nurture and educate – and when it's time to present your offer, they'll be much more likely to take you up on it, as you've been helping them. Even in a worst-case scenario – maintaining your close rate of 30%, say – you've secured nine new clients.

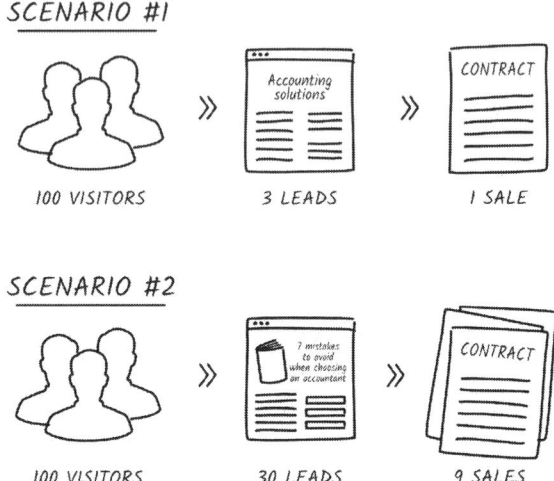

Isn't that amazing? You spent the same amount on advertising to attract 100 prospects, but in the second scenario, you secured nine times as many customers. That's the power of this approach.

In return for your HVCOs' valuable information, you'll be asking customers for their names and email addresses, enabling you to stay in contact with them. It's a simple exchange, but be warned: it only works if your HVCO holds sufficient value.

You can't trick people into receiving a free report that is a promotional piece or a price list in disguise. I'm sure you've been in a situation where you've downloaded a free report, only to be badgered with emails or phone calls pushing a hard-sell message.

HIGH VALUE CONTENT OFFER

That approach leaves people wishing they'd never asked for the information. So, you need to set yourself apart by offering such good value upfront that the customer naturally wants more. To achieve this, follow these simple guidelines:

Rule 1: It must have an attention-grabbing headline

The most crucial part of your HVCO is your headline, which must stop your prospects in their tracks. David Ogilvy, the father of advertising, once revised a headline 104 times before he approved it. And for good reason. On average, eight out of ten people will read the headline but only two will read the content.

Your headline will largely determine the number of people entering your acquisition loop, which is why you should spend just as much time crafting it as you do the content.

I have analysed thousands of headlines and have found that the most successful inspire curiosity.

However, there's a very delicate balance between over-promising and capturing someone's curiosity. Solid headlines never promise more than they can deliver, but can't be so specific that customers feel they have nothing to learn. In other words, your headline needs to be able to deliver the goods, big time. Otherwise, customers feel cheated. Statistically, you're always going to win with headlines that start with the adverb "how" or a number, as they add clarity – but any of these 15 headline formats will have prospective customers scrambling to access your HVCO:

The X best ways to _____ without _____

- The 7 best ways to get rich without a 9-to-5 job
- The 3 best ways to lose weight without dieting

X of the _____ _____ you'll _____

- 11 of the best sunscreens you'll buy at the supermarket today
- 5 of the most diverse companies you can work for

_____ vs _____: Which is _____?

- Playstation vs Xbox: Which is faster?
- Cardio versus resistance training: Which is better?

The unbelievably easy way to _____

- The unbelievably easy way to get the job you want
- The unbelievably easy way to start a business

How to _____ without _____

- How to gain muscle without going to the gym

- How to get your dream job without any experience

How to _____ in_____ without _____

- How to buy a house in the next 12 months without a deposit
- How to drop a dress size in the next fortnight without dieting

The guaranteed method for avoiding _____

- The guaranteed method for avoiding jet lag
- The guaranteed method for avoiding a hangover

X things _____ says about you

- 4 things owning an SUV says about you
- 7 things your hairstyle says about you

X little-known ways to _____

- 7 little-known ways to get rid of rodents
- 9 little-known ways to get a better night's sleep

How to _____ like _____

- How to brand your business like Apple
- How to exponentially grow your business like Amazon

Shocking report reveals the X things you must know about _____

- Shocking report reveals the 5 things you must know about credit card debt
- Shocking report reveals the 7 things you must know about car insurance

X lessons I learned from _____

- 3 lessons I learned from consulting
- 7 lessons I learned while losing weight

The ultimate guide to _____

- The ultimate guide to SEO
- The ultimate guide to building your business

X little-known facts that could affect your _____

- 9 little-known facts that could affect your wealth
- 7 little-known facts when starting a business

How to _____ in _____

- How to write a video script in less than 10 minutes
- How to secure a new client in the next 3 days

Rule 2: Your content needs to be unique, valuable and not publicly available

An HVCO answers the questions your customers are desperately trying to solve, but to be effective, its content must be unique, valuable and not publicly available. If your customers can get the same information from your website or through a web search, your HVCO will not be compelling enough to generate action. I can't emphasise this enough – the content has to hold real value if it's going to compel the customer to exchange their name and email address for it.

Rule 3: Keep it simple

Even though your customers might be asking complicated questions, your response should be pitched in a way that guarantees interaction and comprehension. Or, as Einstein supposedly put it, "Everything should be made as simple as possible, but not simpler."

CHAPTER 8

SELF-LIQUIDATING OFFERS

HVCOs are a proven approach to generating leads, but until a customer buys from you, they can't completely comprehend your offer. Until then, they're left trying to evaluate if the promises you're making about your product or service are true.

So, while an HVCO aims to reduce a customer's uncertainty through information, your self-liquidating offer (SLO) attempts to do this in a different way – by allowing them to experience your products or services via an introductory offer.

Introductory offers are low-cost/high-value products or services created specifically to attract first-time customers to your business. In most cases, it'll be something you splinter off from your core product or service, but sometimes it will require you to create a completely new product or service.

Before buying a car, you'd give it a test drive, right? Think of an introductory offer the same way. It provides your customers with a sense of understanding and experience before they commit to buying your core product.

The crucial thing to note here is that your introductory offer is not intended to solve your customer's whole problem. Rather, it should solve a specific part of it – one that holds enough value for them to want to take the next step with you.

And while creating your introductory offer can be a challenge, a common blunder among entrepreneurs is to disregard many of the steps a customer makes before deciding to buy. That's because they're stuck in the mindset of having to sell immediately – or, to put it another way, they're so focused on selling the car that they completely undervalue the test drive. If they shifted instead to the idea of getting customers ready, the appeal of introductory offers would be much more obvious.

Whatever you choose to use, this is the first time you're asking your prospective customers to get their wallets out, so you need to offer as much value as possible.

Done correctly, an introductory offer's conversion can be as high as 90% – and let me tell you, these are the hottest leads you will ever get. Unlike everybody else, you're showing them the path to their desired outcome and you're proving you can help them. The end result is that they feel they've got a much stronger connection with your brand, meaning the path towards future purchases is significantly smoother.

Introductory offers are a proven, predictable way to acquire an endless supply of new customers. But what I'm about to reveal is how to turn these simple offers into the greatest acquisition system in modern business.

You see, acquisition costs have risen more than 50% in the past five years as marketing has become more expensive and customers have become less trustworthy of brands. It's therefore no surprise that reducing this cost is the most commonly cited marketing priority.

No business has an endless supply of cash to spend on attracting new customers, which is why we need to transform your introductory offer into a self-liquidating offer.

Self-liquidating offers monetise your introductory offer with the sole purpose of repaying the cost of initially acquiring the customer.

For instance, say you allocated $500 to Facebook advertising. Unless you can find more money, your growth is going to stall once that's been spent, because you can't afford to promote yourself any longer. An SLO changes everything, however.

With an SLO, you sell your introductory offer with the explicit goal of regenerating your $500 from its sales. Then, once the $500 is back in your bank account, you can go out and buy more advertising with it repeatedly across the year. It's a never-ending cycle that never stalls, as long as it's done properly.

SELF LIQUIDATING OFFER

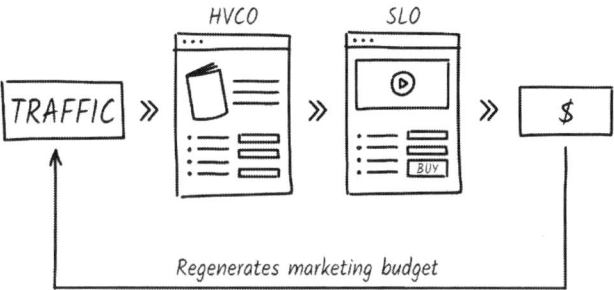

I'll say this loud and clear. If you've ever wondered how to generate more customers than you could ever imagine, this is it.

Let me give you an example of one of my SLOs in action, because it's in your hands right now. This book is my self-liquidating offer. The money you spent on it will be used to regenerate my advertising budget so that I spend it, again and again, attracting more and more customers.

Personally, I won't make a cent from the sale of this book. What I do get is a regenerating advertising budget and an ever-expanding opportunity to work with clients like yourself, which is a million times more valuable to me.

And while an SLO is your secret weapon in growing your own business, it's also highly effective at squashing your competitors' efforts.

For example, say you had a competitor with an advertising budget that was six times larger than yours: for every ad you could afford, they'd be able to buy six. The sad fact is that they will outshout you in a busy marketplace and win every time.

But an SLO can destroy their budget advantage without costing you an additional cent. Your competitors will allocate an advertising budget annually, most likely based on their turnover. They might tweak it now and then, but the advertising budget they set at the beginning of the financial year is essentially what they have to work with.

In contrast, an SLO will keep regenerating itself. It's like having an advertising budget that you get back every time you spend it.

The measure of how fast you get your money back is called your earn-back period. The shorter this is, the faster you'll get your advertising funds back.

So, if you had an advertising budget of $10,000 that you were able to regenerate every two months, you could spend it six times a year. Your total advertising spend would be $60,000, derived from $10,000 you've recycled.

The net result is that you can match a competitor's spend that is six times larger than yours. What's even better, though, is that while your initial $10,000 is the last investment you'll need to make, your rival will have to spend $600,000 over a ten-year span.

On the whole, it's a neat way to destroy your competitors. They can spend their advertising budget only once, while you can spend yours repeatedly.

CHAPTER 9

ONE-TIME OFFERS

An SLO will get your prospects reaching for their wallet for the first time – and if you play your cards right, it won't be the last. We're moving these customers along the trust/uncertainty spectrum. Once they've purchased from you, they'll become exponentially more likely to buy from you again. So, immediately following your SLO, we're going to make another sales offer called a one-time offer (OTO).

Getting someone to make an additional purchase hot on the heels of their first one isn't an easy task. But consider this: your customer is in a state of momentum and still trying to solve their problem. It makes sense to try to sell them the next step as soon as possible.

To cut through their inertia, a standard offer isn't good enough. Instead, you'll be using scarcity and urgency to give them a compelling reason to purchase. Customers will have one chance only, and the purchase must be made instantly. There's no second chance.

Your OTO should complement your SLO purchase with minimal overlap between the two offers, and it must be an essential step towards solving their overall problem. From experience, the best-converting OTOs promise accelerated results or provide a significant risk reduction.

When it comes to accelerated results, your offer will generally consist of a product or service that is complementary to your core product. For instance, if your SLO was an eight-week fitness course and your core service a one-year membership, your OTO might be a course on nutrition that's designed to speed up the results a customer could achieve.

In the case of risk reduction, the focus is on discounts, deals, special gifts or rewards as an incentive to spur your customers into action. This approach is particularly effective when the price difference between your SLO and your core product/service is large. Say, for example, the eight-week training course was selling for $97, and your one-year membership cost $997. Here, your OTO might be a 40% discount on annual membership to bridge the pricing gap, provided the customer takes immediate action and purchases it there and then.

Whichever approach you use, your goal should be to make your offer so irresistible that those who missed out on the opportunity would be disappointed. Be warned, though, that 99% of businesses will put together an offer that isn't compelling enough.

Think of it like this. If I offered to sell you one of the latest mobile phones at full retail price – and you had a phone already that you weren't planning on upgrading – you'd decline. Far from being irresistible, my offer wouldn't overcome your inertia.

But what if I said: "OK, I'll sell it to you for $50"? What would happen? You'd very likely buy the phone, having turned your nose up at it a minute ago.

What's the difference? I've made my offer irresistible. That's what you need your OTO to be. I've given you an extreme example, but hopefully you get the idea of how such an offer works.

To create an irresistible OTO, you'll need to brainstorm ideas about what you could sell. Jot them down as they come to mind, no matter how outrageous they are. Then go through each idea and ask yourself: "Could I confidently deliver this?" Narrow your list down and pick one idea to start with.

Keep in mind that the value to the customer has to be completely out of this world and that you're only going to present this offer once, to a new customer. It must be an exclusive, standalone promotion that your customer can't access anywhere else. Anything less and it loses all credibility.

That doesn't mean you can't sell the same product or service on an ongoing basis; it just means that it can't be the same deal. For instance, your OTO could be a specific product with a 40% discount. You can sell the same product on your website or in your store, but it can't be at the same discount or it'll invalidate your OTO.

ONE-TIME OFFER

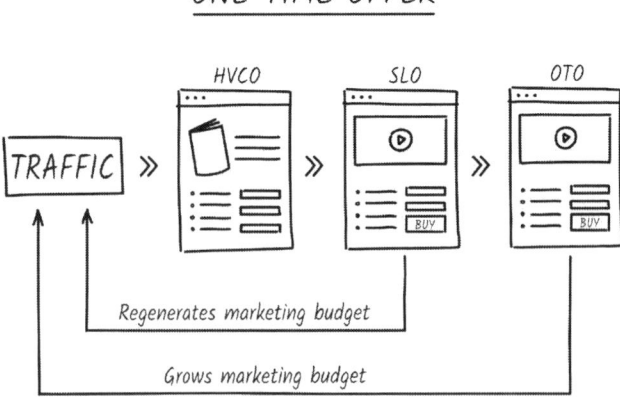

Now, the reason we offer an OTO in the first place is that it plays a very strategic role in your acquisition loop. Firstly, if your SLO can't break even, the profits from your OTO should be used to help regenerate your marketing budget. Reaching self-sufficiency should be the primary objective of your acquisition loop, so if you're struggling, utilise your OTO profits to support this.

If your SLO is breaking even, however, then the profits from your OTO should be invested in your marketing budget. It's not enough to regenerate it; you also need to increase it. That's because as your marketing budget grows, not only will you be able to outperform competitors in the channels you're currently using, you'll also be able to start using new channels that had been too expensive before.

So, there you have it. The net result of your HVCO, SLO and OTO combo is a self-sustaining growth system that continuously builds upon itself.

CHAPTER 10

ACQUISITION LOOPS

Make no mistake, perfecting an acquisition loop is no easy feat. And if there's one absolute truth I can share with you, it's this: whatever you do the first time, it's not going to work.

Less than 1% of all businesses rolling out a growth loop for the first time will succeed immediately, so you've got to be prepared to continue working at it. Your acquisition loop is the holy grail of growth and, like most things we want in life, securing it requires a lot of hard work and determination. The good news is your initial failure will set a benchmark that allows you to judge if you're moving closer to success or further away from it. And that's critical.

We've covered the individual offers that make up the acquisition loop, so let's recap the entire loop to drive home how it transforms a stranger into a paying customer.

It's worth remembering that 3% of your customers should power through your entire loop – so if you've built it correctly, you should see money flowing in immediately. But that leaves 97% of prospective customers floundering somewhere. In that case, your first challenge is to identify who the prospect is and where they're positioned in the loop.

The HVCO – which, as you'll recall, exchanges your valuable content for their name and email address – will tell us who they are. The next step is to determine where they are in the loop

ACQUISITION LOOP

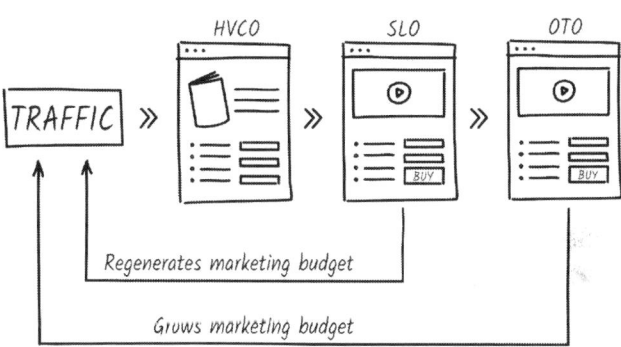

This may seem impossible, but it's actually straightforward, because our only practical option is to present our offers within our acquisition loop to see if they purchase it or not. The moment they decline an offer, we know that they weren't ready to progress and by extension, where they are in the loop.

Let's run through an example so you can see how it works in practice.

IMPLEMENTING YOUR ACQUISITION LOOP

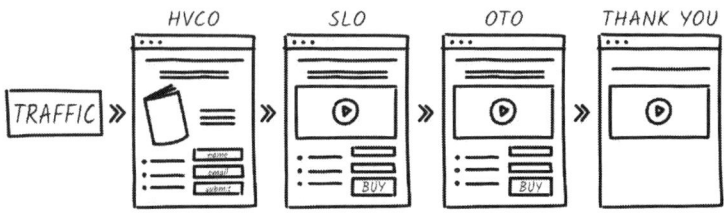

A transformative process

To start, we need to drive prospective customers into your acquisition loop, which we can achieve through traffic sources such as advertising. Say you're using display ads to promote your ebook, "How to Buy a House in the Next 12 Months Without a Deposit".

A prospect who clicks on your ad will be directed to your HVCO landing page, where they can access your content by entering their name and address on a form. This page performs best if it contains only text and an image of your HVCO, so keep it as simple as you can.

Once the prospect hits the submit button, you take them to your SLO page. This should include a video so that you can begin personalising your offers; it's a fantastic medium in terms of conveying emotion and humanising your message. In your video, it's imperative that you acknowledge the success of the submission straight away. Then you can pitch your SLO.

Typically, you'll say something like: "Thanks so much for ordering my ebook 'How to Buy a House in the Next 12 Months Without a Deposit'. It's full of ideas that can help you into your own home in no time at all. It'll be on its way to you shortly, so keep an eye on your inbox. While I have your attention, I wanted to let you know about our _____ "

At which point, you present your self-liquidating offer.

A cold prospect will leave without taking you up on your offer. Then again, you have their contact details, so you can start nurturing a relationship with them by email.

If they took you up on your SLO offer, you'll need to get them to enter their payment details.

Then, once they've filled in the purchase form, you want to take them to your one-time offer page. Again, it's crucial to acknowledge that their purchase of the SLO is confirmed.

"Thanks so much for your purchase of _____, we'll be getting that packaged and on its way to you in the next _____ days," you might start by saying.

Then: "Before you leave, I just wanted to let you know about a special one-time offer that could accelerate your results by _____. It's only available here and right now. And once you leave, you won't be able to access this offer anywhere else again, so please hear me out and you can decide for yourself if it is of interest".

It's time for your OTO. If they don't take you up on it, they'll leave, but you now know where they are in your loop and can nurture them accordingly via email.

If they did buy your OTO, you'll need to process their payment and redirect them to a final thank you page. Here, a simple video should reiterate what they've purchased and the kind of results they should expect. Thank them for their purchases and you're done!

And that's how you build an acquisition loop.

Notice the simplicity of how it turns strangers into paying customers. How it devotes time to educate them and answer their questions. How it removes risk by allowing them to step up their purchases. How it takes cold, warm and hot prospects and categorises them into groups so you can nurture them accordingly. And perhaps most importantly, how it allows you to build a relationship with your customers based on trust and certainty.

These acquisition loops are so powerful that they will transform your business utterly. Anyone who can get theirs running successfully will be able to build a seven-figure business easily, in no time at all.

CHAPTER 11
ASCENSION LADDER

To make speedy progress, you don't have to take huge leaps.

The Japanese call this philosophy Kaizen, which translates as "continuous improvement" or "change for the better". Kaizen achieves success through small, consistent steps, which is the best way to overcome resistance – provably.

Growth loops anticipate the steps required to achieve business growth. But to determine which products or services we'll offer at each step, we use the ascension ladder.

Essentially, the ascension ladder helps you figure out how you're going to take your customer by the hand and in price terms, lead them upwards – from your free offers to your premium-priced offers.

Customers have to enter the ladder somewhere, and while we always design the ladder to start at step 1, that's not necessarily where they'll choose to start. Once they're on our ladder, though, we always want them to go up.

When we talk about customers coming into the ladder, we're referring to traffic that's been driven to our business, generally through advertising.

ASCENSION LADDER

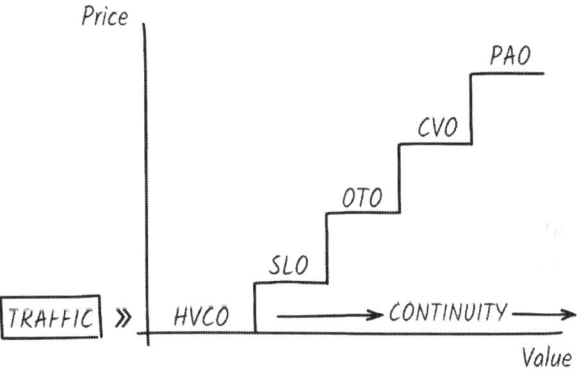

Struggling businesses tend to think their biggest headache is a lack of traffic, but getting traffic isn't as hard as they imagine. Indeed, being able to buy traffic readily is one of the greatest opportunities for a business in the 21st century. More often than not, the real difficulty is picking which option to use from the many available. If you've ever wondered whether to do SEO or paid advertising, social media or content marketing – the list goes on and on, frankly – then you're not alone. With so many competing options and vastly different cost structures and results, the choice can become paralysing.

Yet regardless of the channel you choose, traffic comes in three types only: traffic you buy, traffic you earn and traffic you own.

Traffic you buy

Buying traffic (ads) is the fastest, most reliable way to grow your sales consistently. If you buy sufficient traffic each month, you're controlling the flow of fresh prospects into your business. Over time, you'll discover exactly how much you need to achieve certain revenue levels. Spend more and you'll grow. Spend the same and you'll stabilise your turnover.

Traffic you earn

Traffic you earn is a slower growth strategy but still powerful. This generally requires sweat equity invested over time, and so consistency is key. There are lots of ways to earn traffic, but your choice generally comes down to social media, YouTube, SEO, blogs, etc.

I won't advise businesses against a traffic-you-buy strategy, given how quickly you can achieve results from it. But if you're a bootstrapped business that can't raise enough of a marketing budget to buy traffic, then traffic you earn is where you should start.

Traffic you own

While it may be a phenomenal way to grow your business, buying traffic has one distinct disadvantage: whenever you want more, you have to spend more money.

That's why traffic you own is the most important type, because there are no costs to access it. You don't have to pay Google or Facebook, or do SEO or buy offline ads – you own it already.

That gives you the opportunity to sell to these customers repeatedly, with no additional marketing costs in terms of reaching them. For some businesses, the ability to tap directly into this stream of customers will be the difference between making a profit or not.

The lesson from this is clear, and of monumental importance. Whenever you buy or earn traffic, your primary objective should be to convert that anonymous flow into an identified prospect. That means collecting the customer's name and email address.

It follows that the first step in an ascension ladder is an HVCO, based on the provision of information in exchange for contact details. Customers may obtain information from various sources, but as I've explained, your HVCO should answer their burning questions with unique, valuable content that is not publicly available. Moreover, it helps to establish you as a trusted expert.

The next step up the ladder is your self-liquidating offer (SLO), by which prospects "experience" your products or services. By monetising this, we can regenerate the marketing costs initially spent on acquiring the customer.

After that comes your one-time offer (OTO), an upsell that delivers accelerated results – and by ploughing some or all of the profits from this into growing your marketing fund, you can acquire even more customers.

Combined, these steps create our acquisition loop. A self-sustained system that is continuously building upon itself and is, without a doubt, the smartest route towards growth in modern business.

However, your ascension ladder extends past our acquisition loop. The upshot is that once you've acquired a customer, you need to move into your monetisation loop.

Monetisation loop

Broadly speaking, the monetisation loop is how you're going to make a profit and fund the continuous improvement of your products and services.

Until now, we've focused on the acquisition loop – a process we use to get customers to your monetisation loop. In this way, we've moved the customers closer to their desired outcome, step by step, and as a result, we've bolstered their trust and desire to do business with us. The friction that could have hindered the purchase of our core product or service has been eliminated, so now it's time to present them with your core value offer (CVO).

Your CVO is the offer you're going to make that completely solves your customers' problem. Better still, it won't require a hard sell. You've build a tremendous amount of brand equity, trust, value and goodwill with your customers, which means that when they're ready, of course they're going to buy from you.

But what happens once they've bought your CVO? My guess is that as things stand, this is where you stop trying to sell to them. That's a mistake, because in reaching this point, you have built up a ton of trust and momentum. What's more, a number of customers would be willing to spend more to keep working with you – I guarantee it. This is why, following on from your CVO, you'll be providing a premium ascension offer (PAO).

Given that most of you won't have offers at this level, I imagine offering a premium product or service is something you've dreamt about but haven't developed. However, the question you ought to ask yourself is: "What's the next thing I could sell to someone who has just brought the most expensive thing I currently sell?"

Trust me, there's always an unexplored opportunity waiting for you.

The most common PAOs are things like events, retreats, high-end coaching, workshops and so on, but anything with a high level of customisation and/or exclusivity attached to the offer would fit the bill. For example, one of our clients – a local yoga business – designed a three-day retreat in the mountains that focused on yoga and wellness. Normally, places in their classes cost $30. On this occasion, places on the retreat went for $2,000 a person.

Continuity

The final element of your ascension ladder is a continuity offer, meaning anything you could charge for on a regular basis. Subscriptions, retainers, memberships, check-ups, monthly coaching sessions and storage are good examples.

Offers like these are commonplace, from your computer antivirus subscription to your favourite movie or music streaming app. And if you can't find a continuity plan in your business, I'd argue that you haven't been looking hard enough.

Still struggling to come up with anything? In my experience, the starting point for most clients is to create a paid VIP program with tons of added value for customers who enrol in it.

A real-life ascension ladder

Now that you have a general understanding of ascension ladders, here's a real-world example that shows how easy it is to create one.

A good friend of mine runs a small local gym and one day, he said he'd recently done some advertising and had only managed to sign up two new customers.

When I asked what his offer had been, he explained that it was a 12-week total body transformation program including gym membership, a personalised nutritional plan and a weekly, hour-long personal training session.

It seemed like a great offer to me, so I asked him who he'd targeted. Because of the gym's location, he said, they tended to attract office workers who wanted to lose a bit of extra weight. Interestingly, this group often felt self-conscious about joining a gym because they weren't in shape already.

I wanted to know how those who'd overcome this fear had managed it. After a bit of thought, he said that once the customer was in the gym, their concerns evaporated and they became more focused on their goals.

"So, if getting them in the gym solves that, what could you offer them?" I asked

"Well, we already offer a free trial, but it's not a very successful approach either."

"OK, that doesn't make sense," I said. "Are there any restrictions attached to the free trial?"

"No, that's what I don't understand. They have full access to the gym and they can try out any equipment they like."

"Ah! So, if they've never been to a gym before, or at least in recent years, how are they meant to know how to use the equipment, what weights to do, what reps to do?"

"Well, it's not hard to figure out. But I can see how that could be intimidating for someone who doesn't know what they're doing," he said.

"OK... So, with that in mind, how could you change your offer to address that?"

"Maybe we could create an introductory program specifically for people who haven't been active, to get their body used to exercising again. And when they come in for the first day of the trial, we'll take them through the program and show them all the equipment they'll need to use."

"Awesome," I said, but I still wanted to know how he planned to engage people who'd shown no interest in his offer.

After pondering this for a while, he declared that if people didn't take advantage of a free trial, then nothing would bring them into his gym.

"OK," I said, pressing on, "but before someone was ready, they weren't ready. That raises the question of how you can connect with those that aren't ready yet, but could be one day.'

He looked puzzled. "Why would I want to?"

"Because this is how you build a predictable flow of prospects into your business every month. You need to be constantly warming up the prospects so that when they're ready, you're at the top of their list."

"OK," he said, suddenly more interested. "How would I do that?"

Perhaps, I suggested, a new video on social media each week, containing a fitness hack or a nutrition tip.

"Or perhaps you could create some downloadable articles?" I continued. "Something like 'five things to consider before you join a gym' or 'four exercises that burn fat fast – guaranteed'. Anything that would trigger interest and build your following."

"Awesome. I can see how that would work."

"Yeah," I said, "but we're not done yet. What do you plan to sell to customers who have bought your total body programme?"

The ideal situation, he told me, was that the client would set new goals at the end of the 12 weeks and start a new round of exercise. "But our core offer is our year-long program."

"OK, great. And what would you later sell the customers that sign up for the year-long program?"

He looked downcast. "I don't know. I've run out of things to sell."

I disagreed. It seemed to me that he'd been so focused on keeping money coming through the door that thinking bigger hadn't crossed his mind.

"What could you offer that really excites you?" I asked.

He considered this for several moments until suddenly, a smile spread across his face.

"I'd love to make an exclusive retreat. I could book out a small private resort somewhere and do a high-end, three-day fitness retreat."

"Perfect! But now you need to think about what you could offer to provide some extra stability to your cash flow. The way I see it, the moment you start worrying about cash again, any thoughts of running a private retreat will disappear out the window. You need a continuity program, where you're getting regular payments."

"Oh, that's easy," he said. "I've been thinking of offering this for a while. Accountability is the key to achieving results, so my idea is to provide a bi-monthly executive health check where we do a key biometric and musculoskeletal assessment. It would create a new revenue stream for us."

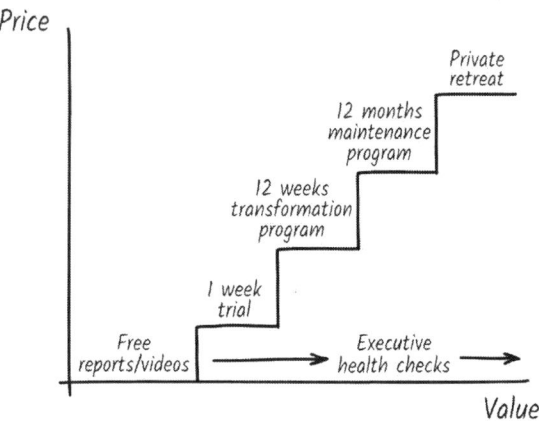

GYM ASCENSION LADDER

And there you have it – that's how easy it is to build an ascension ladder!

Just remember that at each step of the value ladder, you need to offer insane amounts of value so that clients naturally want to ascend. Each time they do so, it means that your goal of offering inspiring, high-end products and services – while making lots more money, of course – is moving ever closer.

But before you start creating your ladder, let's go over some quick guidelines.

Rule 1. Your value ladder must cover every natural progression towards a purchase

Some value ladders might have three steps while others have eight – it depends on what you're offering. What's most important, though, is that each step follows a natural progression. Don't skip steps or expect your customers to make the leap by themselves. You need to explicitly create the conditions for the prospect to progress.

Rule 2. The value ladder must proceed in the right order

The top of the ascension ladder is where you provide the greatest value. How you get there is up to you, but you must build steps for your prospects to ascend naturally. Controlling the ascent is crucial, so you must understand where each of your prospects is in their journey.

Rule 3. Provide insane value at every level

At every step, the prospect is evaluating whether the value they're receiving is worth what they're giving up.

In the beginning, that might only be giving their name and email address, but in the steps that follow, it'll be tens of dollars, then hundreds of dollars and finally thousands or even tens of thousands of dollars. As they progress, the value they're experiencing will determine whether they continue or not. With that in mind, you need to ensure the value you're providing exceeds their expectations.

Rule 4: The only information you collect should be that which facilitates the next step

Every bit of information you ask for creates friction, so only ever ask for the minimum details required to facilitate the next step. In other words, don't ask for someone's phone number if the next step requires you to email them. You can always collect more information as the customers move up your ladder. But requiring more details than are needed will only generate unnecessary friction – a sure way to lose customers.

Rule 5: Be flexible

Your value ladder is not static – it's a starting point and it'll need to be updated. As prospects move up the ladder, make sure you're tracking the level of success and the time it's taking for them to progress. If your efforts to move prospects up a step are failing, you'll need to 1) review the value in the next step and rejig accordingly, or 2) review the distance in the next step. Is the leap too large for the prospect? Do you need to add a step in-between?

CHAPTER 12

CUSTOMER VALUE LADDER

Once you have your ascension ladder, you need to calculate how much each prospect is worth to your business at each rung of it. We do this by calculating your customer value ladder (CVL).

Let me give you an example. Let's say your plan is to:

- Use a free HVCO to generate leads for your business.

- Make those leads an introductory offer: an industry report that you're selling for $50. You anticipate that 30% will take you up on this.

- Decide that you won't provide a one-time offer, because your introductory offer is self-liquidating, so skip straight to your core value offer. In this case, you expect that 50% of the SLO customers will go on to buy a $200 custom report.

- Expect that 30% of the CVL customers will go on to buy your premium ascension offer, which is a $750 strategic implementation plan.

Now, this may sound incorrect, but the customers who bought the $50 report at the introductory level are not actually worth $50 to your business.

Why? Because half of them will also buy your core value offer, the $200 report. Therefore a customer's value at your introductory level is the $50 they've spent, plus 50% of the $200 report ($100). So in fact, customers at the introductory level are worth $150 to your business.

Value of customers at the introductory SLO level
= $50 report + (50% x $200) = $150

Moving up the ladder, we know that 30% of customers at the core value level will go on to buy your premium ascension offer. We also know that to get to this level, they had to have spent $50 for the introductory report.

So customers at your core value offer level are worth $50 (for the introductory report), plus $200 (for the custom report), plus 30% of the $750 implementation plan ($225), making a total of $475.

Value of customer at the CVO level
= $50 + $200 + (30% x $750) = $475

At the final level, a customer's worth is the $50 and $200 combined, plus $750 for the premium ascension offer. That's $1,000 for your business.

Value of customers at the PAO level
= $50 + $200 + 750 = $1,000

Now let's continue the process by stepping down the ladder. Before anyone bought the introductory SLO, you were putting out your HVCO – a free report.

30% of prospects who received this went on to buy our introductory offer. Therefore a prospect at the HVCO level is worth $15 to our business (30% of $50).

Value of customers at the HVCO level
= 30% x $50 = $15

CUSTOMER VALUE LADDER

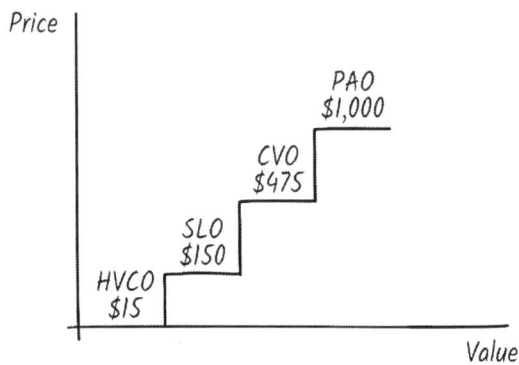

With a complete CVL, we can see how much our customers are worth at each stage, which determines how much we can spend acquiring them.

If our HVCO costs more than $15, then our ladder will fail because it costs us more to get these customers than they're worth to us. That means we'll need to adjust our inputs, such as increasing the cost of the introductory offer, or working to improve the conversion rates.

You'll need to monitor these figures as they change all the time, but the true benefit of the customer value ladder is understanding what you can spend at each step.

CHAPTER 13

PRODUCT/MARKET FIT

To boost your business, you'll need to zero in on those most likely to benefit from using it.

Understanding the customers you're selling to is key to its success. And while defining them can sometimes be difficult, it's an essential undertaking because people buy from people.

How, then, do you identify your ideal customer?

In traditional marketing, we create a persona – that is, a fictional character profile of your dream customer. This includes data such as customer demographics, behaviour patterns, motivations and goals. The good news is that they can provide tremendous structure and insight for your company. The bad news is that in most cases, they're created incorrectly.

The classic mistakes that clients make are creating a dream board filled with images of who they want their customers to be, or, even worse, creating a persona with no usable value. The level of insight in something like "John is married with three kids and lives in a quiet street in the suburbs" isn't actionable.

Thankfully, there's a solution. Rather than building your persona on fantasy or fluff, you want it based on your product/market fit customers.

Product/market fit is a common concept in high-growth companies, but it doesn't seem to have caught on in the rest of the business world yet. That's a shame, as it can inspire new ways to approach growth.

A p/m fit customer understands the value of your offering entirely and is willing and able to pay for it. To demonstrate this, we need to undertake a customer cohort analysis, which is a measure of how your business retains customers over time.

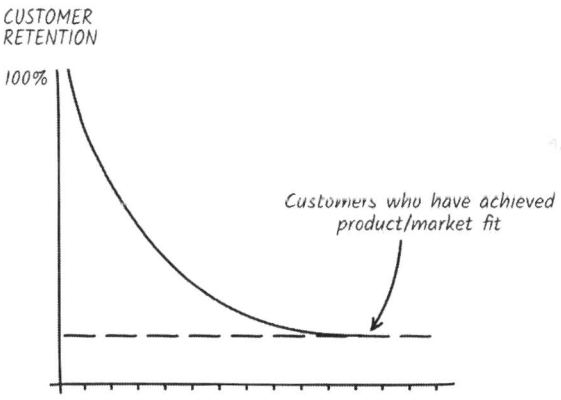

PRODUCT/MARKET FIT

CUSTOMER RETENTION

100%

Customers who have achieved product/market fit

For example, say you acquired 50 new customers in January and then for the rest of the year, you tracked how many you'd retained each month. An initial drop-off is natural, but hopefully you'll see the curve flatten out at some point.

Under that flattening curve are a group of customers that are sticking with your business. They have clearly found value from your products or services, so it's fair to say that they have achieved product/market fit.

The question you need to ask is: "How can I get more of this type of customer?"

To build a deep understanding of this specific sub-set — of customers who recognise the value you're providing and want to keep buying from you – you can start by compiling basic data such as age, location, gender, roles and responsibilities.

On top of that, try to figure out what their problems and aspirations are and how your products or services can help them reach their goals.

You don't need to commission a huge research report or devote endless hours to this task, as a simple four-step approach will give you more than you need.

Step 1: Online research

With two or three major keywords or search phases connected to your products or services, you can tap into a plethora of valuable customer insights.

- Search Google. Join Facebook groups. Read blogs, FAQs, Amazon reviews, Reddit, YouTube comments, LinkedIn forums, Quora and other websites that your p/m clients frequent.

- Make use of auto-suggest. You know how, as you type into a Google search bar, it presents a list of words and phrases it predicts will match your query? It does this with aggregated data, so it's presenting the most searched terms.

- Check out answerthepublic.com, one of the industry's best-kept secrets. Type in your keyword or search phase and it will generate a diagram of related searches.

Step 2: The pain-versus-pleasure principle

It's said that the ability to understand someone's motivation is a superpower in business. At the same time, by analysing the language they're using, you can form a hypothesis about what is motivating their behaviour.

Conceptually, all behaviour is motivated by the pain and pleasure principle, which asserts that everything we do is about seeking pleasure or avoiding pain.

Someone moving towards pleasure might say:

- I want to spend more time with my family.
- I want to be able to show off my new body this summer.
- I want to holiday on a tropical island.

Whereas someone moving away from pain might say:

- I hate my job, so I'm going to start my own business.
- I hate being overweight, so I'm going to start a diet.
- I'm not happy in this relationship, so I'm going to leave.

Evaluate the language used. What's the dominant feeling? Are they moving towards pleasure or away from pain?

When you're creating offers, your copy can tap into this insight, allowing you to win hearts and minds.

Step 3: Interviews

Once you have a broad list of insights from your online research, and a theory about what's motivating them, you need to explore these directly with your p/m fit clients.

Arrange an informal chat over coffee. Explain that you want more clients like them, so you'd like to understand the value they're deriving from your product or service. What are they happy with? What are they unhappy with? What are their concerns and questions? What sort of barriers have they encountered? How does your product/service meet their needs? Why do they stick with you?

Step 4: Direct observation

You should have a solid understanding of your product/market fit customers by this point, but you'll need to back that up with observation.

Watch them use your product/service and work out whether they achieved the desired outcomes they mentioned. Did they become frustrated or excited at any time? Follow the steps they took to achieve their success and how they overcame any challenges. In addition, compare their path to a newly acquired customer and ask yourself how it differs.

Knowing your p/m fit customers will change everything, from your product offering to the tone of your advertisements.

Learning what people want, understanding how you can help them and communicating with them persuasively is how you'll grow your business.

CHAPTER 14

SETTING VALUE, NOT PRICE

The first thing anyone does when comparing products and services is to look at the price difference. It's a crude, elementary comparison because while nobody likes to pay more than they have to, price tells only part of the story.

In reality, consumers buy based on perceived value – the difference between the perceived benefits they expect from a purchase and the perceived price that they pay for it.

Think of perceived value as a calculation that we run in our mind every time we want to make a purchase decision. It helps us maximise the value we're likely to receive when choosing between competing products and services.

When the perceived benefit of a product is more than the perceived price, then a customer is more likely to purchase. Benefits are "perceived" because in the end, the value lies in the customer's mind. What is valuable to one person may not be valuable to the next.

Interestingly, price is also perceived differently from person to person. Say I need a new ink cartridge for my printer. I search online and find that a local store sells it for $50, but there's a store on the other side of town where it's $35. Some people will happily drive across town, while others will see the time and distance involved as too much of an additional cost.

To illustrate perceived customer value, we use a concept called the value map, which expresses the relationship between perceived benefits and price.

VALUE MAP

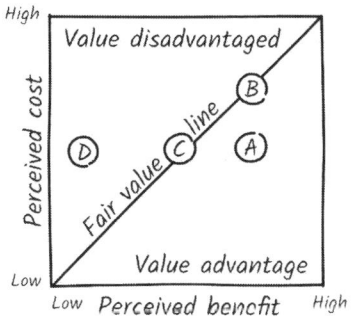

The horizontal axis represents the perceived benefits, the vertical axis is the price and the diagonal line is known as the fair value line (FVL). Businesses that fall below the FVL are said to be in a "value advantaged" position and will be increasing their sales; those that sit above it are "value disadvantaged" and will be in trouble.

If a customer wanted to buy a product with benefits that fall within the range of A and B, then they're more likely to choose A, as it provides the same level of benefits as B but at a lower price.

Alternatively, if a customer had a fixed budget that fell within the price range of A and C, they would likely choose A over C, since A provides greater benefits than C but at the same price. The opposite is true for competitor D, which is in a value-disadvantaged position and will be losing market share.

To illustrate this further, let's consider an example.

HOTEL EXAMPLE

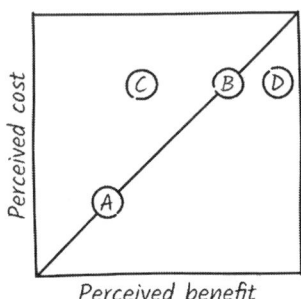

Perceived benefit

In the bottom left quadrant, we have Hotel A, a two-and-a-half-star hotel that charges $100 a night. It offers a nice, clean room with a comfortable bed, but is on a noisy road on the outskirts of town and lacks an onsite restaurant.

In the upper right quadrant, we have Hotel B, a five-star hotel that's $350 a night. It has well-appointed rooms, friendly staff, a central location, expansive views of the city and a top-rated restaurant onsite.

Clearly B offers substantial benefits over A, so it's able to charge more.

Now imagine there's another five-star offering, Hotel C, across the road from B. This has the same facilities as B but its staff are rude, poorly trained and disengaged. In most customers' minds, this would reduce the perceived benefits and move C off the fair value line.

As C loses sales, it has two options to get itself back on the fair value line and improve its occupancy rate: drop its prices or overhaul its service delivery.

Moving off the fair value line is where a lot of enterprises come unstuck, because the change of value happens in the customer's mind. Businesses that don't monitor these changes are often left dumbfounded as sales decline.

But being on the FVL doesn't mean you're outperforming your competitors – it just means you're competitive. To outstrip them, you must move into what's known as a value-advantaged position.

Going back to our example, imagine there's another five-star hotel that has all the facilities as the others and charges the same rate (Hotel D). At the same time, it's in a better location, right on the city's beautiful waterfront, and is surrounded by restaurants and tourist attractions.

This hotel isn't on the fair value line any more as it's delivering greater customer value than the competing five-star hotels. In all likelihood, it would sell out well before the others.

The point I'm making is that to achieve greater sales, you need to move your business into a value-advantaged position. You need to increase the gap between the perceived benefits and the perceived price by making some simple adjustments, but you will need to be smart about how much you vary these attributes.

One tactic you should try to avoid (even though it's the most commonly used) is to lower your price.

Why? Because it erodes your profit margins. And with depleted funds, you'll be unable to support growth efforts such as advertising, bringing on new team members or making product improvements. That makes substantial growth over the long term really hard.

Let me make this clear: the only time lowering your prices makes strategic sense is when you're able to offer the lowest price in your market. There is no competitive advantage to being the second-cheapest.

Here's another example. Say I want to buy a specific mobile phone, so I head down to my local shopping mall, which has three phone shops. The phones are identical, but retailer A has the cheapest price.

Retailer A: $800

Retailer B: $807

Retailer C: $815

The second-cheapest retailer is only $7 more expensive, but why would I spend more for the same product?

If you can't be the cheapest, it's pointless being second or third, or any position after that - except for the most expensive. When executed correctly, there is a massive advantage in being the most expensive, and anyone can achieve that – you just need to put your prices up.

But here's the thing. If you increase your price but the perceived benefits stay the same, then the perceived value drops, driving away customers. The solution is to use the funds you've gained from charging more to boost the perceived value.

This is what most entrepreneurs don't comprehend. If you can't be the lowest-priced business, then perceived value is your battleground.

Perceived value encompasses everything that adds value from the customer's perspective. In short, it comes down to how good your offer is.

Offers

Your offer is the strategic structuring of your products and/or services to create a distinct market position – and as you add more benefits, what you're selling becomes more unique. At the point where it's genuinely one of a kind, you no longer have to compete on price because customers can't get the same level of value anywhere else.

Offers come in two forms:

- Offer stacks sweeten your normal offer by bundling additional products and/or services to boost the perceived value.

- Risk reversal takes as much risk as possible off the customer's shoulders, using policies such as money-back guarantees, warranties or payment plans.

To demonstrate how we build offers, let's head back to the phone example, except this time we'll look at it from the retailers' perspective.

- A, the lowest-priced retailer, was selling the phone for $800 and sold 50 in a day.

- B, the mid-priced retailer, was charging $807 and picked up 15 sales.

- C, the most expensive of the three, sold five phones at $815 each.
- So, in terms of total sales, they turned over $40,000, $12,105 and $4,075 respectively.

Retailer:	A	B	C
Sale price:	$800	$807	$815
Units sold:	50 sales	15 sales	5 sales
Sales:	$40,000	$12,105	$4,075

Clearly, the lowest-priced retailer is taking the lion's share of the sales. If Retailer C wants to compete, then it needs to create an offer that increases the perceived customer value.

Subsequently, C does this by including a protective case with each phone, three screen protectors and a screen replacement warranty if the phone is damaged within a year. This is what we mean by an offer stack.

Naturally, these additional elements come at a cost, but that might be as little as $10 when sourcing directly from a manufacturer. To the customer, though, the perceived value could add up to $150.

They think: "Well, for an extra $15, I'm getting $150 worth of stuff! Only an idiot wouldn't take up that deal!" So, the offer has moved Retailer C into a value-advantaged position.

Retailer:	A	B	C
Sale price:	$800	$807	$815
Units sold:	25 sales	5 sales	21 sales
Sales:	$20,000	$4,035	$17,115

The lowest price is still very appealing, so Retailer A will continue to pick up a large share of total sales: 25 per day. But Retailer C has created an offer that competes at the other end of the price spectrum and is achieving 21 sales a day. Amazingly, its sales turnover has increased 400%.

Building an offer requires a bit of imagination and ingenuity, but it doesn't need to be complicated. You just need to figure out what is going to increase the perceived customer value.

And to figure that out, we use the process of offer hacking.

CHAPTER 15

BUILDING YOUR OFFERS

The first step in creating your offer is to look at what you could include to increase its perceived value. The key to this is offer hacking, a process that involves finding out what's already working in the marketplace and creating your own version of it, with some improvements.

To be clear, we're not talking about directly copying a competitor. We're talking about figuring out what's working for them, then combining it with your own ideas to create something that's distinctly yours.

A lot of entrepreneurs think that offer hacking is more complicated than that, but it isn't. You don't need to reinvent the wheel to have something that outsells your competitors – it just needs to have greater perceived value than theirs.

To start with, you need to identify the competitors you'll be analysing. Some will provide products or services that compete directly against yours, but keep in mind that there'll be indirect competitors that solve the same problem from a totally different angle.

Say, for example, my product is a weight-loss supplement. I'm competing head-on with other weight-loss supplements, but also indirectly with gyms and nutritionists.

Naturally, you'll want to know what's driving the success of your most accomplished rivals. Smaller competitors are often forced to innovate faster to survive, so you might find some gems hidden away there too.

Once you've completed a list of competitors, you should find out what they're selling, how they're selling it, how they're pricing it and how they're getting their messages out to the market. That way, you can draw your own conclusions about what's working for them.

On a practical level, you need to browse their website, sign up for newsletters/promotions and go shopping in their stores. And to experience how they sell their products, I'd encourage you to buy from them. If you're shopping on their website, take screenshots as you progress through the sale. Note the headlines they're using to grab your attention and the copy they're using to justify the sale.

Are they bundling their offers? Providing bonuses? How do they price and discount? Is there any sign of them using an ascension ladder? How did they follow up the sale? These are the types of questions to ask, because everything they're putting into the marketplace is evidence of their winning sales formula.

As you're collating this information, bullet point the elements that make up their offers. Then add any ideas you may have and write them down, no matter how ludicrous they seem.

The next step is to split your ideas into three categories:

- Information
- Products/services
- Risk reversal

Information

Facts, directions, statistics, data and instructions all count as information, as does anything else that is of value and communicated. Not only is it a great means of increasing perceived value, it can also be done at low cost. A how-to video, for instance, costs money to produce, but after that, you could distribute it for years with no extra outlay.

Let's think again about that weight-loss supplement. We could add in a complimentary video training programme or a book with 100 healthy recipes. Beyond that, perhaps a 12-week ebook challenge, a private support group on Facebook or individual consultations via Zoom.

Physical products or additional services

As the name suggests, this is anything that you could bundle in with your offer. If our weight-loss supplement comes in powder form, that could mean a free mixer bottle. Alternatively, we might consider training bands, a free T-shirt, a skipping rope or a cap. An additional service might take the form of an app that reminds them to take their supplement, or perhaps a free online consultation.

Risk reversal

The aim of risk reversal is to relieve the customer of as much risk as possible. Examples of this are a 30-day money-back guarantee if they don't see any results, or a payment plan that lets the customer experience the benefits of your product immediately with minimal financial risk. Perhaps they pay 30% upfront and 70% when they achieve the results we've promised them; or maybe it's low-interest finance that's easy to apply for.

Reviewing your options

The objective of this brainstorming process is to have a whole range of ideas, even if some of them sound silly at first. You'll choose from these ideas as you construct your offers. But if you can't realistically and consistently deliver what you're proposing, now's the time to throw that idea away.

You don't have to use every idea either; just enough to create the level of perceived value you're aiming for. That might be a single item or a bundle, depending on the circumstances. Just remember that as you add benefits, what you're selling becomes more unique to your business – so in general, the more the better.

BUILDING YOUR OFFERS

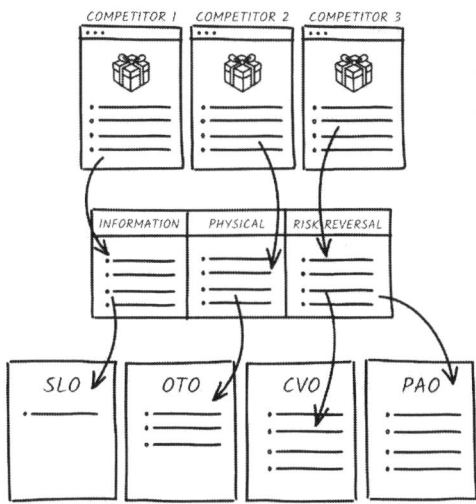

Create your self-liquidating offer first. Your goal is to regenerate your marketing budget from this, so it needs to hold enough perceived value that it induces the customer to take action. Often, the SLO will be one of the best things on your list.

Once that's decided, you need to build your one-time offer, allocating an element or elements from your list as you do so. Your OTO is an upsell that uses the principle of scarcity and urgency, so select these elements accordingly.

After that, apply the same approach to your core value offer and premium ascension offer.

Value stacking

As you add elements to your offers, you need to track their perceived value so that the sum exceeds the cost.

To be effective, you should aim for a multiplication factor of ten, meaning for every $100 of perceived value you plan to deliver, you should not be spending more than $10 on add-on elements. As this can be harder to achieve with physical products, information-based elements are often preferable.

The value stack works on the principle that the only thing your prospect will remember when you're trying to sell to them is the last thing you showed them. For most sales presentations, that's going to be the final price, but what we really want them to keep top of mind is the value they're deriving from your offer.

To do that, you need to state and price each element so that your customer can clearly associate the full value you're providing.

VALUE STACKING

By this juncture, you're almost ready to take your offer to the world. But before you do that, you'll need to know how to present it.

CHAPTER 16

HOOK, STORY, BRIDGE, OFFER

At the heart of all of your offers is the messaging you'll be using to attract customers' attention and persuade them to buy from you.

Copywriting is a critical skill because it's salesmanship in writing. Indeed, it's the primary tool you have to persuade customers to move from one step to the next.

The universal sales approach to copywriting is to make your customers aware that a problem exists, show them you have a viable solution and convince them to purchase it.

Every time you create an offer, your messaging needs a structure to maximise its effectiveness. This four-step formula generates great results, in any industry, regardless of your businesses size or target audience. It works across any format, too, whether it's your website, Google Ads, sales letters, cold calls, webinars, live events, newspaper ads or pay-per-click ads, including those on Facebook and YouTube.

So, what are the four steps?

1. **Hook** – Attract people's attention.

2. **Story** – Get them to trust and believe in you with a story that appeals to their emotions and makes them want to engage with you.

3. **Bridge** – Create the link between your story and your offer.

4. **Offer** – Provide them with your offer.

HOOK, STORY, BRIDGE, OFFER

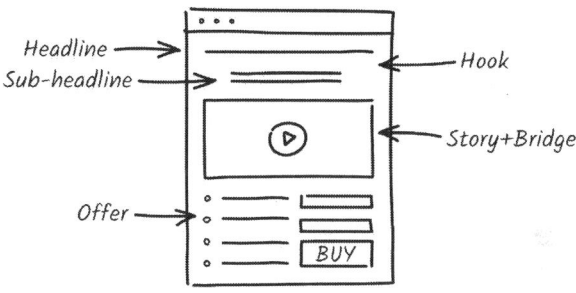

Step 1: The hook

Did you know that the average consumer now has an attention span of only seven seconds? That's two seconds less than a goldfish! We live in a world of constant demands and distractions – not least when it comes to advertising, which bombards us endlessly.

It's estimated that we're exposed to more than 4,000 advertising messages a day, and the bad news is that unless you're doing something groundbreaking, most of your marketing is completely ignored. That said, it's not especially difficult to gain consumers' attention. All it takes is a little more creativity and effort.

Why is this important? Because understanding and managing attention is the single most important determinant to business success. If you want to succeed in this economy, you've got to be good at getting your customers' attention.

To do this, we use hooks – typically short, bold headlines, though they can also be videos, images or even questions. A hook's purpose is to interrupt whatever people are doing (reading, watching, listening, scrolling or surfing) and focus their attention on our message.

Think of the last time you were scrolling through your Facebook or Instagram feed and something captured your attention. Perhaps it was a picture of an athletic person with a six-pack of abs with a headline that said something like "Lose 10kg for $10", or a photo of someone on a private yacht, entitled "How I made $1 million working from my laptop". These are examples of hooks.

Finding a hook that works isn't easy. In fact, it's probably the hardest part of the selling process. Once you've found a hook that works, however, it's your golden ticket to growth.

Step 2: The story

Stories are one of the most powerful tools you can use to engage and connect with your audience. As well as relaying facts and data, they can incorporate an emotional element that gives greater depth and meaning to our messages.

Stories can reframe problems as challenges, which makes the message more relatable. Perhaps more importantly, they can calm our customers' sales detectors so they're more receptive and open. No one likes being sold to, but everyone enjoys a good story.

Let me give you an example:

Target audience: Business owners who are struggling to get new clients

Hook: How I doubled the size of my business in just 60 days!

Story: I'd always dreamt of owning my own business, so three years ago, I left my full-time job and launched my company. It was both exhilarating and terrifying taking the leap, but I was committed, so I invested every cent I had into it. I worked every hour I had to get it off the ground, and although it wasn't easy, within 12 months the business was profitable. But then it happened. A major client left and my company turnover dropped 50% overnight. I only had enough funds to last two more months, so I desperately started cold calling potential clients. The problem was they had no idea who I was or how I could help them, so I didn't have any success. I wasn't sure how I was going to save my business until my friend gave me a book about providing growth loops. This taught me a simple selling system and over the next two months, I secured three new clients, saving my company from closure.

Step 3: The bridge

The bridge is equivalent to the moral of a story and is used to create a link between the story and your offer. This is a crucial step because without a moral, your story is basically meaningless and won't drive change. What you will find is that many of the details in your story don't really matter once the bridge is revealed. The only parts that do will specifically relate to the bridge, so go back to your story and remove any irrelevant content.

Depending on the offer we want to present, any of these bridges would be suitable for the example I've mentioned:

- *"Which got me thinking about how I could help other business owners, so I..."*
- *"But after experiencing stress like that, I knew that my health had suffered, which is why I..."*
- *"My point is when you're down, it's hard to see a way out, but there is a way. Sometimes the solution comes from the most unlikely source, which is why I..."*

Step 4: The offer

This last step will lead to either a purchase or an action. You need to spell out exactly what the customers will get, what they will pay and what their next step is For example, if our bridge was "Which got me thinking about how I could help other business owners", our offer could be:

So, I'd like to invite you to my free one-day event where I'll show you how you can triple your sales in just 60 days. I'll personally take you through my seven crucial steps, and by the end of the day, you'll have a bespoke plan that you can start implementing immediately.

- *All-access VIP ticket $297*
- *Three break out rooms for deep-dive strategic planning $99*
- *Workshop book "7 crucial steps to triple your sales" $47*
- *Bespoke training specific to your business $497*
- *Total value: $940*
- *Cost: FREE!*

CHAPTER 17
TRAFFIC

When it comes to generating traffic for your ascension ladder, we've mainly discussed the use of paid advertising. Still, there's a vast amount of alternative options to choose between that might make more sense for your business.

Your options can either be proactive or passive.

Proactive traffic generation requires some form of effort – cold calling, networking functions or trade events, for example – where you're required to physically turn up and generate interest in your product.

By contrast, passive traffic generation can happen without your involvement – for instance, if you were to hire someone to do your SEO or run your social media campaign.

By splitting your plan into proactive or passive options, you're ascertaining which channels are going to require your time and which are going to require your money. It's often the case that when you have one of these, you don't have the other, so you need to determine where you sit on that spectrum. There's no point selecting cold calling if you're too busy to call anyone. Likewise, there's no point choosing paid advertising if you don't have the cash for it.

Furthermore, you'll need to consider short-term versus long-term allocations. For instance, you might plan to start with SEO and Google Ads, but then drop Google Ads later on if your SEO is generating sufficient traffic.

Lastly, you'll need to be confident that your choices will bring in enough customers. If you plan to generate 500 leads from a networking function that only 50 people are attending, you're going to run into trouble hitting your goals.

A vast number of traffic generation channels exist, and with more popping up every day, your choice isn't getting any easier. However, these are the most common options at present:

1. **Search engine marketing** (SEM) enables companies to advertise to customers searching on Google and other search engines.

2. **Social and display ads** on sites such as Facebook, Instagram and hundreds of others.

3. **Offline ads** such as TV spots, radio commercials, billboards, newspapers and magazines.

4. **Search engine optimisation** (SEO): the process of ensuring your website shows up high in the rankings for key search results.

5. **Content marketing**: producing valuable content to acquire customers.

6. **Email marketing**: one of the best ways to convert prospects while retaining and monetising existing customers.

7. **Viral marketing**: encouraging customers to spread the word about your business.

8. **Partnerships and business development**: creating strategic relationships that benefit both you and your partner.

9. **Engineering as marketing**: using engineering resources such as microsites, widgets and free tools to acquire customers.

10. **Cold calling**: making an unsolicited visit or phone call in an attempt to sell.

11. **Affiliate marketing**: marketing through others with a similar target audience to promote your product to their audience.

12. **Trade shows**: a chance for companies in specific industries to show off their latest products.

13. **Offline events**: sponsoring or running offline events, from small meetups to large conferences.

14. **Speaking engagements**: leverage a speaking event to promote your product or service.

15. **Community building**: creating a community for your customers to interact with one another.

16. **Resellers, distributors and brokers**: external parties that sell and distribute your product.

17. **Publicity:** the art of getting your name out there via traditional media outlets such as newspapers.

18. **Unconventional PR**: doing something exceptional, like a publicity stunt, to draw media attention.

19. **Referral marketing**: using an existing customer to refer a new customer to your product.

20. **Directories and lists**: leveraging the influence of other companies to promote your product through their lists.

21. **Influencer outreach**: leveraging the influence others have on your target audience and getting them to promote your business.

22. **Bought outreach and guest blogging**.

23. **Retargeting** an audience that has shown interest in the past.

Once you've mulled over these options, you need to allocate one or two channels that you think have the greatest chance of moving the sales needle, bearing in mind your resources (time and/or money).

Now, calculate how many leads you'll need to generate the sales turnover you're after and allocate a target to each traffic option. Say you need 500 new leads a year to hit your sales target, and the channels you've chosen are display ads and cold calling. If you reckon you could generate 50 leads from cold calling, that leaves a target of 450 from display ads.

Next, you need to test your strategy, so buy some display ads and allocate some time towards cold calling over a specific week. At the end of that period, review the results, make any changes necessary and then roll out another test. The goal is to keep refining your activity until you can profitably acquire a customer from it.

Then, once you're getting a positive return on investment, you should roll those additional profits into trying out a new channel. If you start with SEO, say, and find after six months that you're getting an acceptable return on investment from it, then roll these profits into something else, such as Facebook ads.

Ideally, you should end up with at least three sources of traffic, but ensure you get each one running profitably before you add to them. If something bad happens with one source, like the cost suddenly spiking, shift the budget to an alternative source while you figure out how to get the affected one back to its original volume.

CHAPTER 18

LANDING PAGE VERSUS WEBSITE

A s its main gateway, your website sets the tone for everything your company has to offer. It introduces visitors to your brand, your products, your services, your values, history, team, contacts, plus tons of general information. It's their first impression of you.

However, it needs to accommodate a broad audience, which leads to relatively generic messaging, multiple page goals and tons of links and buttons. The problem is that all of these elements come at a price: distraction. And when it comes to making sales, those distractions chip away at your success.

Simply put, websites can't do it all. This is why you're going to use landing pages to manage your offers. Landing pages zero in on one conversion goal, giving you more control over where and what your visitors do. In short, landing pages are designed for conversion, while websites are designed for informing and directing traffic.

Imagine that a webpage is a bucket and the traffic you're sending to it is water. A "website bucket" has multiple holes in it, which allows conversion "leaks", so you lose water (traffic) in all directions. It's called the paradox of choice: the more options you have, the harder it is to make a decision. In contrast, a landing page bucket has one hole drilled into the bottom, so the stream of water naturally flows through that specific hole (sales).

A landing page completely customises a visitor's experience from the moment they click on an ad through to their moment of conversion. By sending people to a landing page customised to match the ad, with a targeted message, cohesive design and a single call to action, you're delivering the experience your customers expect from that initial click. It's that focused experience that leaves less room for pause, fewer chances for distraction. That in turn creates more opportunities to sell your offer.

LANDING PAGE

Landing pages should contain everything a visitor needs to evaluate an offer quickly, and nothing more. That's what makes them so effective at converting. They emphasise content with a simple layout.

Eye-tracking studies show that web visitors will view the main image or headline first. They'll then check the subheadings before glancing down the left side to look for bulleted or italicised text. Body copy will be read last. This is known as the F-shape pattern.

To get readers to comprehend your offers, you'll need to create what is called a visual hierarchy. It should consist of these elements:

1. Use attention-grabbing images and a big headline to grab your readers' attention.

2. A subheading that restates your offer and what they're getting.

3. Compelling bullet points that explain how your product/service is going to help your prospect.

4. Body copy that provides a deeper explanation.

5. Opt-in (for your HVCO) or purchase form (for your other offers).

LANDING PAGES

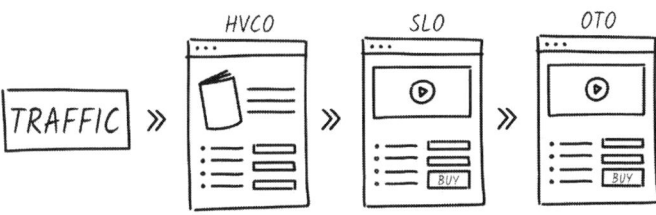

The first landing page your prospects will visit is your HVCO page. This has the single purpose of capturing people's contact details in exchange for your HVCO.

Once they've signed up, they'll automatically be re-directed to your SLO landing page and then your OTO landing page.

The best part of this set-up is that once we have their details and we know where they are in our loop, we have the ability to follow up and nurture these prospects via email. Surprising as it may seem, that's how you'll make the majority of your sales.

CHAPTER 19
EFFECTIVE EXPOSURE

What I'm about to reveal is one of the most effective profit-generating tactics I've ever discovered. In fact, it's so persuasive that you'll have paying customers banging on your door demanding to buy your products or services in no time at all.

It's called "effective exposure" and it's depicted as an S-shaped curve.

Effective exposure is the optimal number of times a person needs to see your offer before they'll take action and buy. Many business owners think that if someone looks at their ad and doesn't buy, that person wasn't interested. They couldn't be more wrong.

As consumers, we're constantly tuning out advertising messages. At any given moment, we can't pay very much attention to more than a few things — there's a term for this: spotlight focusing. And unfortunately for us entrepreneurs, our offers fall outside of that focus most of the time.

Having said that, sometimes an offer will slip into that spotlight, and getting our prospects to notice ours enough will make them more likely to buy. Repeating an offer until it's been noticed is crucial, because it pushes prospects over a threshold.

EFFECTIVE EXPOSURE ZONE

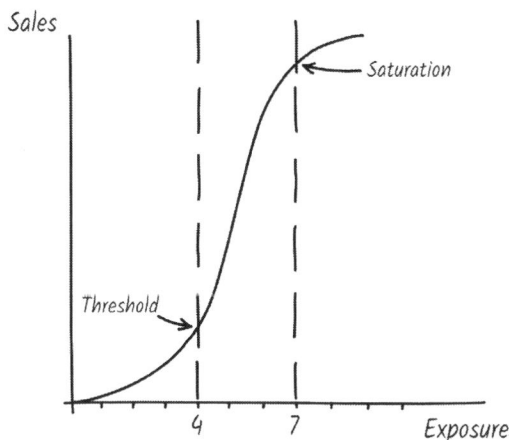

The S-shape captures the notions of threshold and saturation. Below the threshold, there's little impact on sales, because your prospect has barely been exposed to your offer and so there hasn't been enough stimuli to generate to action.

At the other end of the curve is a point of saturation, however, where additional exposures won't help sales either. At these levels, your prospects would have seen your offer so much that eventually, they become insensitive to the stimuli. And so, continuing to try to get your offer in front of these prospects becomes a costly and rewardless effort.

Thankfully, in the middle of the S-curve is a golden zone where each additional exposure boosts sales.

When you're connecting with prospects here, it resonates.

Effective exposure – or as it's known in advertising, effective frequency – has historically been quite controversial, as the goal has always been to define it as a specific number. The ad world has declared it to be "at least three times", based on "Why three exposures may be enough" – an article by General Electric's Herbert Krugman in the Journal of Advertising Research in 1972.

This doesn't mean three is the magic number. Rather, you shouldn't expect much in the way of results without at least three exposures.

In more recent times, marketing psychologist Dr Jeffrey Lant's "rule of seven" has gained traction. Business executive Jay Abraham, reportedly the world's highest-paid marketing consultant, has backed this idea up, citing seven as the number of times you have to ask for a sale before you get a "yes".

After years of extensive testing, I have found that rather than a specific number, there is a zone. And while I agree that seven exposures does achieve the most responses, my research shows that four are the most profitable. In other words, while you can capture sales with more than four exposures, the cost of doing so reduces your profitability.

You should work out your own business's effective exposure zone, but my cardinal rule is that the sweet spot is somewhere between four and seven exposures.

This is why, in the acquisition growth loop, we plan for four exposures – the ad, HVCO, SLO and OTO – before we present our core offer.

And while we do ask the prospect to purchase our SLO and OTO, those offers were deliberately designed to remove risk. It's not until we present our core offer that we ask them to make a purchase decision based on true market conditions.

If you're successfully getting customers through your acquisition loop, you'll only need four exposures. But if your prospect drops out of your loop, you'll need to aim for seven, as they clearly need more stimuli before they'll take action.

Say someone clicked on your ad, exchanged their contact details for your HVCO but didn't purchase your SLO. Given that they've had only two exposures and aren't progressing through our loop, we need a way to deliver five more to get them to the optimal seven.

Advertising is expensive, so we achieve this using email.

The framework we use, called email sequencing, is designed to deliver the five additional exposures. It turns a significant number of fence-sitters into genuine, eager buyers. But it's time-sensitive, so you need to use within five days of somebody joining your list. Its success depends entirely on getting this right – because from a sales perspective, this is where things really get interesting.

You'll get your 3% of customers in "buy now" mode through your entire acquisition loop, but it's the 37% of customers that aren't quite ready that you'll be targeting with email sequencing. And because this group is so much larger, most of your sales will originate from here.

Sequencing may at first appear complicated but just remember that it's merely a written sales conversation with a prospect. Best of all, you can automate this, so once it's up and running, it will do the work for you. All you need to worry about is the torrent of customers insisting you take their cash!

CHAPTER 20

EMAIL SEQUENCING

'll let you in on a little-known fact. In terms of return on investment (ROI), email outperforms every other marketing channel. Every single one of them.

Email is the most direct and effective way of connecting with prospects, nurturing them and transforming them into customers. People who buy products marketed through email spend 138% more than those who don't receive email offers. And according to an American study by the Direct Marketing Association, email marketing has an ROI of 4,400%. That's insane!

If you suspect that social media converts better, think again. The average order value from an email is at least three times higher than the equivalent from social media. Email is the best way to make sales, so if you're serious about growth, it's critical.

Hang on, though. Before you rush off and frantically spam your prospects, let me share another secret with you. A massive one.

When somebody joins your email list for the first time, you must try to establish a relationship with them - before you try selling to them again.

This insight is my secret weapon in email sequencing. It's so simple, yet 99% of business will get it wrong.

Even large-scale enterprises can be clueless, as the following example shows. Recently I bought a new pair of Apple AirPods from a major online electronics store that I hadn't used before. I did so because it was selling them for $50 less than anywhere else. Surprisingly, when I went to pay for the item, they didn't even try to upsell me. All I got was a "thank you" confirmation page.

Wondering how they planned to recoup their lost margins, I eagerly opened the next day's email, which was promoting a range of heated electric blankets. I was shocked. Did their database show that people who buy AirPods are most likely to need an electric blanket too? Shaking my head, I deleted the email.

The next day's email was promoting smart TVs. Delete!

The day after that, microwave ovens. That's when I unsubscribed.

Anyway, here's my point; you should use this form of communication to build relationships. If someone gives you their email address, treat it with respect. Don't bombard them with irrelevant promotions in the hope that they'll buy some random item.

Your prospects are busy people with limited time and money, so don't waste the small window you have with them before another problem demands their attention.

Email sequencing tries to find a balance between this fading attention and our own desire to close a sale through additional exposures.

We can't just approach the prospect for five days and ask if they'll buy our stuff, however. Instead, each email needs to offer more value to draw them up our ascension ladder.

Which brings me back to the electronics store. Do not include anything and everything you have to sell in your emails! The more options there are, the harder your prospects find it to make a decision. Your email sequence should only sell the next thing on your ladder.

Let me say that again, because it is crucial: your email sequence should only sell the next thing on your ladder.

And because we'll be talking about the same offer for five days, we need to approach it in a particular order.

Day 1: Welcome

Day 2: Background

Day 3: Breakthrough

Day 4: Benefits

Day 5: Urgency

As soon as somebody joins your list, send them a welcome email that says hello and explains what your business does. Whatever you do, though, don't write it like some pesky sales brochure. Informality, even humour if you can pull it off, will make you much more relatable.

Your next email needs to spell out the background of your product/service – specifically, the circumstances and challenges you faced before you created it. Also, include a link to a video that reveals a "secret", following the same process you used to produce your HVCO. This "secret" is the first step in terms of adding value to your prospect.

Your third email will recall your breakthrough moment, when you realised you had or could create a solution that others could benefit from, and will contain a link to a video that reveals a second secret.

In your fourth email, point to the benefits that customers are getting from your product, service or business – and while you're at it, add a link to a testimonial video that supports these claims.

By this point, you've laid the groundwork for a relationship. You've told your prospect what your business does, how you came to create your product or service and how it solves the problem the customer is facing. You've provided third-party proof that supports your claims, plus you've shown them two "secrets" videos that prove you're capable and trustworthy.

Now's the time, in email number four, to try a sales offer. If they make a purchase, then you don't need to send the day-five email. You've achieved your objective.

However, if they haven't purchased by the end of day four, there's only one tool left for us to use.

Urgency.

This is our last push to convince them to take action. And as we discussed in the OTO section, whenever you use urgency, it must be real or you risk losing credibility.

What I've found works best is a bonus offer that expires that day. All being well, they'll buy from you – but if they don't, you should retract your offer.

EMAIL SEQUENCING

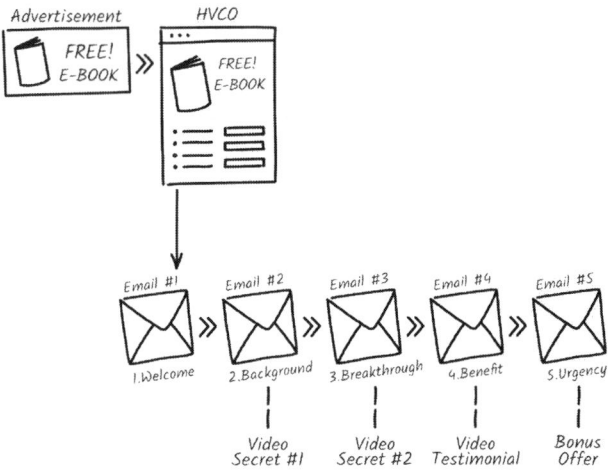

And that's it. A battle-tested approach to smashing your sales targets.

But before we move on, you'll need to master a writing technique that will create so much intrigue, your prospects will barely be able to contain their excitement.

The technique is called continuous narrative, a term typically used for artwork that shows multiple scenes from a story in a single painting or sculpture.

Though there's a clear beginning and end to the story, the scenes inbetween blend and overlap so much that it's difficult to ascertain where one ends and another one starts.

In a similar vein, each email you write must introduce a story that doesn't conclude until the next email.

It's probably easiest if I walk you through an email sequence for my book, where someone has joined my email list by exchanging their details for my HVCO.

Day 1: Welcome

Subject: Welcome!

Hey, this is Matt, and I want to welcome you to the world of growth loops.

For over 25 years, I've helped businesses like yours grow using traditional advertising approaches, and over that time it has become more and more obvious to me that it doesn't work like it used to.

So in the past five years, I've researched how modern businesses are truly growing. What I've discovered is a framework that can double the size of any business, regardless of the industry they're in.

And now I'm sharing what I've learnt.

Tomorrow I'm going to send you an exclusive video that explains the secret of never having to spend another cent on advertising while still outspending your competitors. Sounds impossible, right? It'll make more sense tomorrow...

Look for the email then!

Thanks

Matt

PS. Make sure you open my email when it comes. The subject line is "I had to close my business down".

Day 2: Background

Subject: I had to close my business down

"How did this happen?" my wife asked as tears formed in her eyes. I looked down again at the pile of unpaid invoices on my desk.

Ten years of blood, sweat and tears, and now my business was broke.

"What do we do now?" she asked.

I looked back at her and smiled. "We're going to rebuild it. But this time, we're going to do it right."

And so, we did, but how we did it and the results we achieved will blow you away.

In tomorrow's email, I'm going to reveal the first thing we did and how you could easily do it too.

So, look out for tomorrow's email. The subject line is "Sorry, we're not taking on more clients at the moment". (Of course, we'll make an exception for you! haha)

Thanks

Matt

PS. I almost forgot. I told you yesterday that I was going to give you access to an exclusive video that explains the secret of never having to spend another cent on advertising while still outspending your competitors. You can get it here, but please don't share it: [video link]

Day 3: Breakthrough

Subject: Sorry, we're not taking on more clients at the moment

"I'm sorry, but we don't have the capacity to take on new clients at the moment."

I hung up the phone. That was the third client I'd turned away this week.

There just weren't enough hours in the day. And that's when I realised that unless I changed my business model from one-on-one to one-to-many, I was always going to be constrained by the clock.

And so I did the maths. Currently, I was able to help 40 clients a week, but if I wrote a book with the same information, then I could help thousands, maybe even tens of thousands of businesses a year.

And the best thing was, I only needed to create it once.

But it quickly became clear there was one thing that was going to be detrimental to my success.

It turns out it's the same thing for any business wanting to grow.

Would you like to know what it is?

If so, I've just posted a quick video that shows you this one simple idea: [video link]

Thanks

Matt

> PS. Tomorrow I'm going to share with you a few little-known benefits of my system. They're benefits that you probably don't even know about or expect.

Day 4: Benefits

> **Subject: Little-known benefits of the system that will blow you away!**
>
> When I wrote my book, I knew it would help struggling businesses, but what caught me off guard was the transformation of the entrepreneurs' personal lives.
>
> I've received emails, letters and calls, thanking me for giving them the tools that helped them save their marriages, educate their children, provide life-saving surgery and much, much more.
>
> I knew it'd help, but I never realised how much this would end up improving their lives.
>
> But I guess that's what business should really be. A vehicle to help make your dreams, wants and desires become a reality.
>
> That's certainly what Sandra has achieved. After applying the growth loop methodology to her business, she was able to adopt the "laptop lifestyle", which, if you haven't heard of it yet, allows her to travel the world while making an income from her laptop. You should check out her video, but I must warn you ... you're going to get super-jealous! [video link]
>
> If you want more for yourself, your family and your friends, then you need to get a copy of my new book. You can get on Amazon today for $24.95,

but if you buy it through the link below, I'll give it to you for free if you can cover shipping and handling.

Does that sound more than fair?

To claim your free copy, click this link: [link]

Thanks

Matt

Day 5: Urgency

Subject: Last call

Over the past few days, I've been sharing some tips and techniques to grow your business exponentially, but I haven't shared everything.

But there is one place you can find it all – and that's in my new book, which you can get for free if you cover shipping and handling by clicking on [link].

It's already transforming other people's businesses, and I know it can help yours.

If you've got time, you should check out Gary's video [testimonial video]. Gary's business has grown 3,200% since he started using the growth loops methodology. And you wouldn't believe which tactic is working best for him. I'll leave that for Gary to reveal.

In the meantime, I've got a special offer for you.

Last year I gave a special workshop on how to get five high-value clients in the next 30 days. Thankfully I recorded it, and even though the workshop cost $297 to attend, I'm going to give you access to it for free when you buy my book.

But here's the thing, my special offer expires today...

So, if you're reading this email after tomorrow, I apologise.

You've been warned!

Thanks

Matt

This method of nurturing your prospects will flood your business with eager-to-buy customers in no time at all. In fact, it will become your number-one source of new revenue.

Maintenance email sequence

While the five-day introductory email sequence provides you with the best chance of acquiring a profitable customer quickly, sometimes the timing isn't right.

In this situation, we don't want to disappear off the customer's radar completely. So, after the five-day sequence, we keep in touch via ongoing maintenance emails.

Your maintenance sequence will largely consist of updates about your business, product or service. You must always adhere to this rule, however: every email must tie back to whatever you're trying to sell.

This works as follows. Last winter, I started thinking about replacing the wood on our deck at home. At the time it was pouring with rain, so it was far from being an urgent job, but I wanted to understand what it would cost when I eventually got around to doing it. I contacted two suppliers, and once I'd received quotes from them, I explained that it was for a project I'd be doing in the summer, so I didn't want to buy immediately.

That was the last communication I had with the supplier whose quote was cheapest. They probably thought that I would just return when I was ready to buy.

But the other supplier added me to their maintenance email list and began sending regular updates about projects they were working on. These were beautifully photographed, and while the deck was my main focal point, the emails provided additional value with ideas about planting plans, lighting and the use of outdoor sculptures. And while most of the communication was project and achievement-based, they often talked about the challenges and failures they had faced.

Here's one of my favourite emails from them:

> **Subject: We spent $20,000 by accident today**
>
> It's fair to say today was a bad day.
>
> We were placing an order for a beautiful decking wood called heavy hopea.
>
> It's a South-East Asian hardwood timber that is an attractive light to medium-brown colour, that eventually transforms into a driftwood silver if it's left to weather.
>
> And then it happened... A miscalculation with the exchange rate resulted in us accidentally ordering $20,000 worth, instead of the $10,000 we had intended to order.

It wasn't until a few weeks later that we realised the error we'd made, so we frantically called the supplier and explained the mistake.

Unfortunately the order had already been fulfilled and was on its way but to help out he agreed to a 20% discount.

So anyway, we've got twice the amount of this beautiful wood on its way than we need, so if you've got a project that you could use it for, then let's get in touch and we'll pass the full discount on to you.

Thanks

John

Would you ever admit to your customers that you'd stuffed up? Probably not. But by the end of that email, I had discovered a new hardwood that I'd never of before, and I knew that I could get it at a legitimately reduced price.

That's the joy of a maintenance email sequence – you can share whatever you like, the good, the bad and the ugly, as long as it ties back to your offer.

When summer rolled around, we ended up buying some of the heavy hopea for our decking project. The supplier won my business by keeping in touch, continuing to add value and treating me like a friend. That's the winning formula for maintenance emails.

CHAPTER 21

GROWTH METRICS

If there's one fact I know about marketing, it's that you're going to need to make changes to your plan. And to know if those changes are leading to improvements, you're going to need to track growth metrics.

Your growth hinges on two fundamental metrics: customer lifetime value (CLTV) and customer acquisition cost (CAC). These determine how much a customer is worth to you over their lifetime with your business, and how much you can spend to acquire them while still making a healthy profit.

CLTV is the total revenue a firm can reasonably expect to earn from a single customer during their predicted lifespan with the business. The longer a customer continues to purchase from a company, the greater their lifetime value becomes.

Why is this metric important? Let's run through an example.

Say you create ebooks on highly technical subjects for a fixed fee of $1,500. For simplicity's sake, creating these requires only your time. There are no other associated costs.

You run some advertisements that cost you $2,000 and secure one new client. On the face of it, this was a waste of time because you're $500 out of pocket. However, this type of thinking is why most entrepreneurs stay small. They look only at the first sale, rather than the lifetime value.

Consider this. Because the ebook you wrote did such a good job for the client, the customer comes back three months later and buys another from you.

So, now you've made $3,000 worth of sales from this client, which translates to $1,000 profit. On this basis, we'd say that the $2,000 advertising campaign was a success.

Let's extend the timeframe out further. When you review your existing client base, it turns out that on average, a client will purchase three ebooks a year and they'll stay with your business for four years. So on average, over four years, your customers will commission 12 ebooks from you, spending $18,000.

Apply that calculation to your latest client and you'll make $16,000 profit over their lifetime with your business.

Can you see why understanding customer lifetime value is a crucial metric to get your head around? Not understanding simple metrics like this one is what keeps businesses small. You don't want to be the entrepreneur pulling their advertising when they make a $500 loss. You want to be the one that understands the true worth of each client, so any money invested in gaining a client is an investment in your business's future.

Now that you've grasped its importance, let's look at how to calculate CLTV.

Customer lifetime value model

1. **Calculate your average purchase value:** Divide your business's total revenue in a time period (usually a year) by the number of purchases over the course of that period.

AVERAGE PURCHASE VALUE

$$APV = \frac{TOTAL\ REVENUE}{NUMBER\ OF\ ORDERS}$$

2. **Calculate your average purchase frequency rate:** Divide the number of purchases by the number of unique customers who made purchases during that period.

AVERAGE PURCHASE FREQUENCY RATE

$$APFR = \frac{NUMBER\ OF\ PURCHASES}{NUMBER\ OF\ CUSTOMERS}$$

3. **Calculate your customer value:** Multiply the average purchase value by the average purchase frequency rate.

CUSTOMER VALUE

$$CV = \frac{AVERAGE\ PURCHASE\ VALUE}{AVERAGE\ PURCHASE\ FREQUENCY\ RATE}$$

4. **Calculate your average customer lifespan:** Work out, in years, the average length of time a customer purchases from your company.

AVERAGE CUSTOMER LIFESPAN

$$ACL = \frac{SUM\ OF\ CUSTOMER\ LIFESPANS}{NUMBER\ OF\ CUSTOMERS}$$

5. **Calculate your CLTV:** Multiply customer value by the average customer lifespan. This will give you the revenue you can reasonably expect an average customer to generate for your company over the course of your relationship.

CUSTOMER LIFETIME VALUE

$$CLTV = \frac{CUSTOMER\ VALUE}{AVERAGE\ CUSTOMER\ LIFESPAN}$$

Customer acquisition cost

Paid advertising is the fastest, most predictable way to introduce new prospects to your business, but it often terrifies business owners because of the high perceived costs associated with it. Frankly, they should worry more about the cost of not advertising.

Paid advertising is a critical component in growing your sales, and over time you'll come to learn exactly how much is required to achieve a certain revenue level. Once you understand this, the fear of using paid advertising vanishes.

Customer acquisition cost (CAC) measures the cost of attracting and converting a prospect into a paying customer. But where CAC is different from standard campaign metrics is that it accounts for all of your marketing and sales costs too.

A standard campaign metric like cost per acquisition (CPA) measures the cost of the advertising channel against its acquisition numbers. Say you spent $1,000 on Google Ads and secured 100 customers, then your CPA is $10. But here's where CPA falls down: it doesn't account for all of the costs associated with making the Google Ads campaign happen in the first place.

That's why we use CAC, because it takes into account all of the marketing and sales costs such as salaries, commissions, bonuses and overheads associated with the task of attracting new leads and converting them into paying customers. All of these are essential expenses, and so CAC provides a more realistic business-level metric.

CUSTOMER ACQUISITION COST

$$CAC = \frac{(COST\ OF\ SALES + COST\ OF\ MARKETING)}{NEW\ CUSTOMERS\ ACQUIRED}$$

To calculate your CAC, the first step is to determine the time period that you're evaluating (month, quarter, year, etc). Then, add your total marketing and sales expenses together and divide that total by the number of new customers acquired during this period. The resulting value is your company's estimated cost of acquiring a new customer.

For example, let's say your company spent $50,000 on sales and $30,000 on marketing on a new campaign, and you generated 800 new customers across the first quarter. Then your cost to acquire a customer for that quarter is $100.

($50,000 + $30,000)/800 customers
= $100 per customer

CAC is much more representative of the true cost of acquiring a customer and ultimately reveals if your business can succeed or not. If your CAC is higher than your CLTV, then your business cannot succeed.

Suppose your CLTV is $400 and your CAC is $450. Your business is destined to fail, as you'll be paying more to acquire a customer than you can make back from them.

It's also important to note how much greater your CLTV is than your CAC, as it tells you how fast your businesses revenue will grow.

For example:

- Company A's CAC is $100 and its CLTV is $400, giving it a CAC:CLTV ratio = 1:4

- Company B's CAC is $2,000 and its CLTV is $4,000, giving it a CAC:CLTV ratio = 1:2

Even though Company B's CLTV is ten times greater, Company A's ratio shows that it can scale twice as fast as Company B.

Aiming for the right balance ensures you're getting the most out of your budgets. Ideally, your CAC:CLTV ratio should be 1:3, meaning the value of your customers is three times the cost of acquiring them. At 1:1, you're spending the same amount of money on attaining them as they're spending with you. But if it were 1:5, say, it may mean that you're not spending enough on sales and marketing and could be missing opportunities to attract new leads.

The other benefit of CAC is that it can also be used at the campaign level. You can calculate the CAC for each of your separate marketing channels, then work out which is best at securing customers cost-efficiently. Combine that with your CLTV and you'll know which channel brings you the most valuable customers overall. Armed with these numbers, it should be pretty obvious which channels are creating profitable customers and which channels are costing you far more than they're worth.

CHAPTER 22
RETENTION

There's only one thing better than acquiring a new customer, and that's retaining an existing one. Why? Because nothing impacts long-term growth more than retention. Nothing.

While its traditional role is to keep your customers coming back, you may be surprised to learn that its impacts on acquisition are just as profound.

In fact, if you're struggling with acquisition, you should shift your focus to retention, given its boundless capacity to deliver growth. In a moment, we'll look at three key approaches:

1. Growth stacking

2. Modification

3. Expansion

First, though, let's get a better understanding of how we measure retention.

Coming back for more

Most businesses think that if they have a great product or service, customer retention will happen naturally. It doesn't.

The harsh truth is that sooner or later, your customers will leave. This is called customer churn, and while it's not the happiest metric, it's vital in monitoring your business's health.

The simplest way to calculate your retention rate is to compare the number of customers you have at the beginning of a certain period with the number at the end. If you have 100 customers at the start of one month and 95 remain a month later, then your retention rate is 95%.

And while calculating retention is a super-simple concept, at the last count, public companies had 43 ways of accounting for the metric.

Making this a complex task is a waste of time and effort, since only two questions matter. Firstly, which timeframe are you measuring? Secondly, is your customer still a customer?

The period you choose should correlate to a customer receiving value. That might be daily for an app, monthly for an accountant and yearly for an apartment rental business. However, the sooner you become aware of retention issues, the better, so generally, monthly tracking is recommended.

Growth stacking

If your business is growing, it's because you're growth stacking. If it has plateaued or is failing, it's because you're not.

So, what exactly does the term mean?

Think of your business as a leaky bucket. Pouring water into the top represents new customers (acquisition).

The water that's now in your bucket represents active customers (retention).

The water leaking out the bottom represents the clients you're losing (churn).

If the hole in the bottom is too big, it doesn't matter how much water you pour in, as eventually it will drain out.

But if the hole is fairly small, then each time you add more water, it begins to accumulate. Your successive gains are greater than your successive losses.

With growth stacking, we're analysing the comparative rate of gains against losses.

To see how this looks in the real world, let's compare two gyms – Mason's Gym and Miller's Gym.

Mason's Gym has an acquisition strategy that brings in 100 new customers every month like clockwork. Over the course of a year, the gym tracks its customer retention on a monthly basis and produces a chart like this:

# of new Customers	Month	0	1	2	3	4	5	6	7	8	9	10	11
100	Jan	100%	40%	30%	20%	13%	8%	7%	6%	5%	4%	3%	2%
100	Feb	100%	40%	30%	20%	13%	8%	7%	6%	5%	4%	3%	
100	Mar	100%	40%	30%	20%	13%	8%	7%	6%	5%	4%		
100	Apr	100%	40%	30%	20%	13%	8%	7%	6%	5%			
100	May	100%	40%	30%	20%	13%	8%	7%	6%				
100	Jun	100%	40%	30%	20%	13%	8%	7%					
100	Jul	100%	40%	30%	20%	13%	8%						
100	Aug	100%	40%	30%	20%	13%							
100	Sep	100%	40%	30%	20%								
100	Oct	100%	40%	30%									
100	Nov	100%	40%										
100	Dec	100%											
Average:		100%	40%	30%	30%	13%	8%	7%	6%	5%	4%	3%	2%

Month zero is when it secures the first 100 new customers. After that, it measures how many customers it still has at end of each month. For simplicity, we're going to assume the customer drop-off rate follows a consistent pattern (i.e. 40%, 30%, 20%... etc.)

Looking at this chart, we see the gym has retained only 40 of its new customers after the first month. By month two, that's dropped to 30 and at the end of the year, only two are left, as this line graph shows.

RETENTION COHORT CURVE

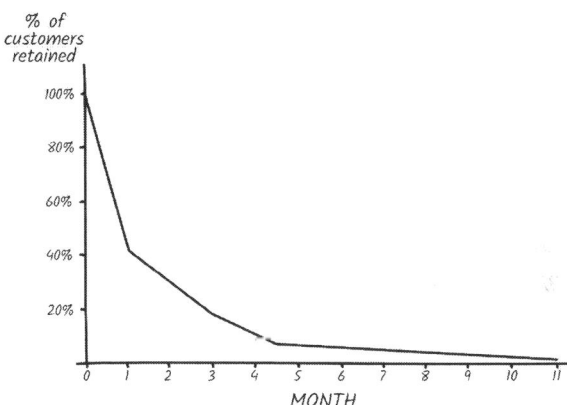

We call each group of customers we're tracking a cohort, which is a fancy word for a group of people with something in common. In this example, we're tracking an acquisition cohort by month and the graph is called a retention cohort curve.

By compiling the data as a chart, we get a much better picture of what retention looks like over time for this business. And what we're most interested in is the shape of the curve.

Every business's retention curve will decline over time, so what we're looking for is whether it flattens. In this case, it doesn't. In fact it's trending towards zero, meaning at some point, this business will churn through 100% of its customers from this cohort.

Churn is the decay of growth, and its accumulation over time will silently kill a business.

To demonstrate this, we stack consecutive monthly cohorts on top of each other.

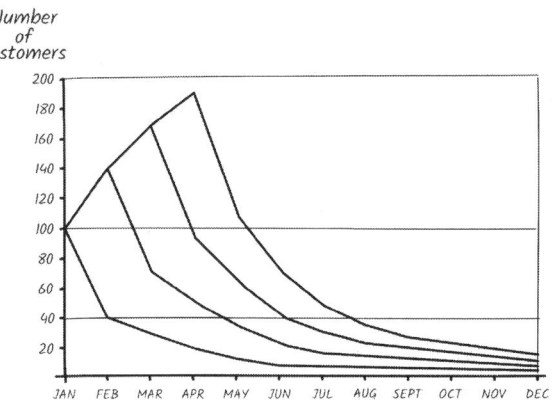

COHORT ANALYSIS

In the short term, the decay is not particularly obvious. The gym had 100 customers in January; by February, only 40 remained, but its acquisition efforts that month secured another 100, bringing the total to 140.

By March, only 30 remained from January's cohort and 40 from February's. Nonetheless, the gym acquires another 100 customers, making 170 in all. This doesn't look too bad on the surface, but the rot that's set in will destroy any successive gains.

To demonstrate this, let's extrapolate this data over two years.

COHORT ANALYSIS - EXTENDED

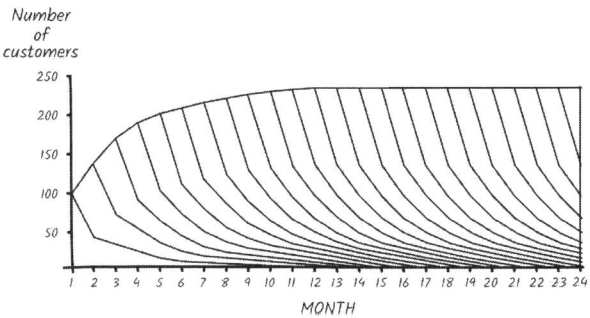

Although the gym continues to secure 100 new customers each month, its growth will eventually plateau as the churn accumulates. In other words, the people it's adding every month won't make up for those who are leaving.

And consider the impact on the gym's revenue.

REVENUE CURVE

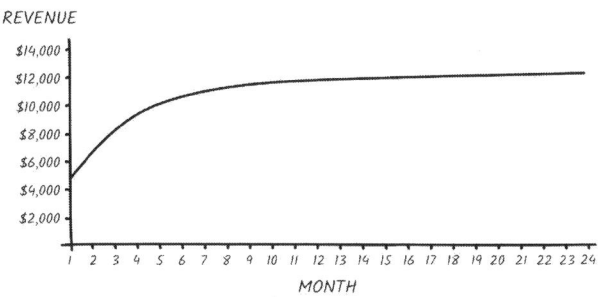

If every customer is paying $50 a month, in time it becomes impossible for the business to earn more than $11,900 a month, even though they're finding 100 new customers in that period! So, what do we end up with? A logarithmic curve where business growth has stalled.

Miller's Gym, by contrast, has flattened its retention curve. It too has an acquisition strategy that delivers 100 new customers a month and, like Mason's Gym, it charges $50 a month. It also loses 80% of its customers in the first three months, the same as Mason's Gym.

The difference is that Miller's Gym gets 20% of its customers into the habit of going there.

FLATTENED RETENTION CURVE

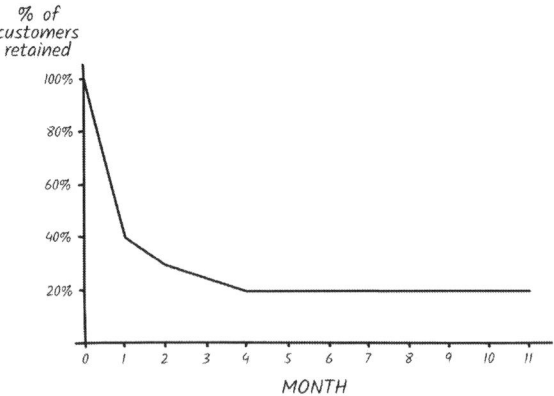

Now, when we stack these cohorts, we get a very different outcome. As a portion of each cohort stays over time, it creates a stacking effect that leads to continuous growth.

COHORT ANALYSIS WITH FLATTENED RETENTION CURVE

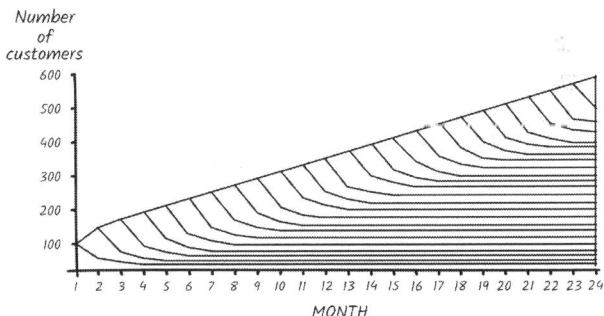

And if that's changed to a revenue curve, we see that the business continues to grow with no plateau in sight. By month 24, it's reached $29,500 in monthly revenue, which is 248% more than Mason's Gym.

REVENUE CURVE

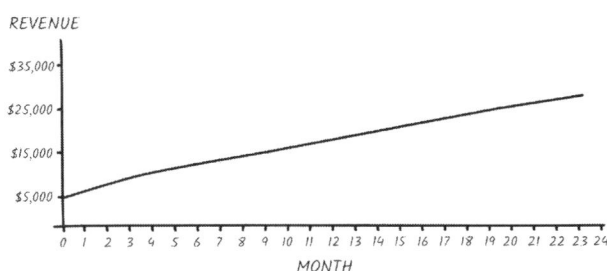

When retention is strong, so is revenue. This is why it's so important to get your retention curve to flatten out as quickly as possible and with the highest possible percentage of customers.

Modification

While the primary goal of retention is growth stacking, it is far from the only benefit.

Retention's impact on acquisition is remarkable because its capacity to create growth is limitless. In fact, it changes the unchangeable.

You see, all acquisition strategies will face some form of constraint, mostly budgetary. But retention doesn't suffer from the same weakness. It doesn't care what the sales and marketing budget is, so it can modify the mathematics of your acquisition strategy.

It achieves this in a variety of ways, most notably by adjusting your customer lifetime value. As your retention rates improve, you're also increasing CLTV because by sticking around for longer, these customers will spend more money. Achieving a modest 5% increase in retention can raise profits by at least 25%, in fact.

Say you have a lawnmowing business that charges customers $50 a month and on average, a customer contracts your services for ten months, so your CLTV is $500. If you double your retention to 20 months, your CLTV becomes $1,000. And as your CLTV increases, your budget for customer acquisition (CAC) increases – meaning you can afford to spend more on acquiring new customers while still making a handsome profit.

Furthermore, as you increase this acquisition spend, you'll naturally start acquiring customers at a faster rate than you could before, and so your earn-back period starts to decline. In effect, every dollar you invest in acquisition is being returned faster. The quicker you can get your money back, the sooner you'll have the funds to acquire even more customers, and so the cycle continues at an accelerating pace.

Expansion

Here's some more good news. Through expansion, retention also improves your acquisition opportunities. We'll define expansion as the likelihood of something being shared and spread to others – so the longer a customer stays with your business, the more chances you'll have to encourage them to spread the good news about you.

Any time a customer recommends your business in the form of referrals, testimonials, social sharing, word of mouth and so on, they're doing that.

But this can also happen indirectly, when a business promotes itself using assets created for customers – for instance, when an architects' firm showcases its designs.

Either way, the more you can positively influence expansion, the more customers you'll gain.

CHAPTER 23
CONCLUSION

W e've covered a lot of ground in this book, and right now you're probably feeling a bit overwhelmed. But that's actually a good thing. Subconsciously your brain will be frantically trying to make sense of it all, and after you've allowed it to settle in for a day or two, hopefully, some clarity will start to form.

The growth loops methodology itself is actually straight forward. It's re-thinking how your business can grow that will be your greatest challenge. Because inevitably, that means you're going to need to change what you've been doing. And with anything new, your first reaction is going to revert safely back to the status quo. But if you're serious about growth, you need to stop doing more of the same stuff.

Throughout this book, I've shared powerful new approaches that when applied, will change your business forever. But all of that information is worthless if you don't take any action.

My advice to you is to get your first acquisition loop up and running as quickly as possible. Don't overthink it or try to reach perfection before you launch it. As I've said all along, your first loop is more likely to fail than succeed, but when you move fast, you fail forward. Figure out what worked and what needs to be improved upon then make the changes that are needed.

As someone who committed to reading this book, you have already proven yourself as an achiever. You deserve this success and can truly have it all.

Matt Berry

PS. When I set out to write this book, I knew it was going to take a massive commitment to see it through. The one thing that kept me going was the anticipation of being able to change people's lives because I know this framework has the power to transform struggling businesses.

When you do succeed, will you do me a favour and tell me all about it? You can send me an email or even a quick video if you prefer.

matt@daringtobegreatbook.com

ONE LAST THING...

Many entrepreneurs and business owners ask me to personally look at their ideas, startups or businesses. I've done it for many of them and they saw dramatic improvements almost overnight. That's what I love about this methodology. You can apply parts of it without much effort, and then see an impact on your sales almost immediately.

But it's becoming harder to accommodate everyone who wants more personalised help, so going forward we're limiting it to a select group and as a reader of this book you have gained automatic priority in our application process.

If you're interested in us helping you build and implement your growth loops, then please apply here: www.growthloops.co.nz/innercircle

I look forward to talking with you soon,

Matt

Made in United States
Orlando, FL
26 January 2022

14071549R00098